Jamie's Watch

For Kevin,
who taught me everything I know
about Jamie

ISBN: 0-9764927-0-9

Printed by Alexander's Print Advantage
Cover design by Melanie Cottam
Layout design by Mindy Sue Brimley
Cover art work by Jeff Brimley

Visit www.jamieswatch.com to share comments
about *Jamie's Watch* or to order copies of the book.

Jamie's Watch

by C. Eric Ott

Prologue

The old pocket watch was clearly unusual.

From the slender, needlelike hands to the elegant Roman numeral face, everything about the ancient timepiece reflected the careful work of some long-forgotten Swiss craftsman. It was thick and heavy, with an engraved gold casing that unscrewed to reveal glittering silver springs and delicate balance wheels. The broad stem was capped by a large round knob that had deep grooves for easy winding.

In an earlier age this instrument had functioned flawlessly, patiently marking hour after hour, day after day, year after year, lifetime after lifetime. Now it lay silent on a desk in Brian Spencer's bedroom, a mute token of the past.

Brian had received the watch from his father, who had received it from his father. No one knew exactly how long it had been in the family, or when it had stopped working.

Once he had taken the watch to a jeweler to see if it could be fixed. The jeweler eyed the watch with admiration. Carefully removing the back, he studied the inner workings through magnifying lenses strapped to his head. "Everything's there," he muttered softly, almost to himself. "Just worn out, I guess. I don't have parts to fix it, and, frankly, I'd be afraid to touch it for fear of breaking something. But I'll tell you what. I'll give you $150 for it, as is."

Brian said no; the watch was a family heirloom and he would keep it. He took it home and put it on the desk in his bedroom by the pictures of his wife and children.

In time, the old watch was mostly forgotten.

Chapter One
April 1983

Brian Spencer stepped back from the lawn spreader and surveyed the results of his work. The grass still had the appearance of a faded shag carpet, but he knew that would change. In a week or two it would be green and springy. Hefting the bag of lawn fertilizer to his shoulder, he took another hopeful look around the yard and headed for the garage. He could see new foliage on some of the shrubs and a few white blossoms on the cherry tree. Spring was definitely on the move. He smiled as he contemplated the advent of longer days and warmer temperatures.

Brian was a big man with balding hair, a round face, and wide shoulders. He was not overweight big—just large big—though the accumulated pounds of recent years had produced a slight protrusion in his mid-section. He looked more like a football player than an English teacher. Ironically, he was both. The football part of him was past tense. He had been a linebacker in high school. He had also played football in college, though his usual position there was on the side line. Still, as he had stated on more than one occasion, the bench was a great place as long as a scholarship was tacked to it. He had made it through college riding the bench.

The English teacher part of him was present tense. High school football player becomes high school English teacher; the theme was intriguing and he wondered if anyone had ever done a movie on it. School teaching was definitely not the most glamorous profession in the world, nor the best compensated. But it gave him a chance to associate with two of his favorite things: books and kids.

Books to Brian were like wires to an electrician. They were the lines that tied his work together, the hands-on part of his profession. Fiction, poetry, and essays gave insight and meaning to his life. A friend once observed that it didn't seem fair that someone could sit around reading novels and stories and get paid for it. While being an English teacher wasn't quite that simple, Brian had to admit that the opportunity to read literature every day was one of the things that kept him in his profession. Like the chapters in his books, his own life was carefully ordered and sequenced. He liked to think of himself as an idea person, a rational, even-tempered sort who used his mind and intellect to successfully navigate the pathways and crossroads of life.

The other half of the school equation was the kids. Less predictable than books, but more promising, it was the students that gave real purpose to his job as a teacher. He liked working with students. He enjoyed watching them learn and grow. He especially relished the challenge of getting them to think. Sometimes they brought sorrow into his life; a few made him downright miserable at times. But when he saw them walk through the graduation arch, it made everything worthwhile. That's when he got his real pay for being a teacher.

There were other kids in his life besides the students: his three children. They and their mother—his wife Marianne— owned more of him than even the high school did. He could visualize himself someday without his English classes, but he could not imagine his life without the people who shared his home. Years ago, when he first decided to have a family, he had vowed to put them first in his life. So far he had been able to do that. And so far, life, if not generous, had been sufficient. Brian didn't require personal adventure. He was more than willing to relegate adventure and conflict to the pages of the novels and poetry that lined the bookcase in his classroom.

Brian opened the back door of the garage and plunged into the cool darkness. Blinded momentarily, he pushed the spreader in front of him as he maneuvered across the cement floor. He found the corner, hung the spreader in its accustomed spot on the wall, and dropped the bag of fertilizer to the floor. Rubbing his hands to dislodge a few clinging fertilizer pellets, he made his way back across the garage and opened the door into the kitchen.

Angela was standing by the sink eating a slice of toast smeared with strawberry jam, the final portion of her late-morning breakfast. The oldest of his three children, Angela at thirteen was on the delicate bridge between childhood and adulthood. She had dark hair like her mother, some of her father's height but little of his weight, and an average-looking face that might have come out of any junior high school yearbook. Among her qualities were ingenuity and determination. She vigorously pursued the things that were important to her.

Right now what was important to her was negotiating a better deal for her Saturday jobs.

"Dad, how come I have to clean the bathrooms again? I just did it last week. Or maybe it was two weeks ago. Anyway, I don't feel like doing it again today. Could I do something else instead?" She looked into his face.

"Gee, honey, I don't know what to tell you about that," he replied, shrugging his shoulders and looking away to avoid the piercing eyes. "Mom's in charge of the job list. I think you'll have to talk to her. I don't even know what the assignments are for today."

"I do. The job list says *you're* supposed to vacuum the living room and the family room. How about a trade, dad? Okay?"

Brian eyed her solemnly for a moment, weighing the relative merits of discipline versus compassion. Angela turned back toward the sink, gazing out the window into the backyard. He walked over beside her. Picking up a glass, he filled it slowly with water from the tap and took a long drink — the drink that had brought him into the kitchen. Carefully replacing the glass on the counter top, he turned again to look at his daughter. Putting his hands on her shoulders and leaning over so that his mouth was close to her ear, he whispered, "Okay, it's a deal." Then, giving her a fleeting kiss on the cheek, he turned and walked away. Out of the corner of his eye he caught a glimpse of Angela clenching her fist and exclaiming "Yes" to herself as he stepped back into the garage.

He paused there just long enough to grab a shovel, then went back into the yard. It was the kind of spring day that made Brian yearn to be out of doors. The air was cool and crisp, but a warm sun more than made up the difference. Snow topped the mountains in the Colorado landscape behind the fence, and the ground was still moist, but the white stuff was all gone from the valley. A few weeds had sprouted in the borders around the edge of the lawn. These were the object of Brian's immediate attention. Grasping the shovel with his left hand in the middle of the shaft and his right hand at the top, he bent over and slashed at the weeds, cutting them down from behind and below. While many prefer the hoe for uprooting weeds, Brian was a shovel man. He had experimented both ways and had methodically concluded that shovels were more efficient in the long run.

In any case, it didn't take long for him to dispatch the few little sprouts that had dared to invade his back yard so early in the season. They bowed to his blade like bowling pins in a championship match. Soon he was leaning on the shovel handle and looking around for another excuse to remain outside. As soon as he went indoors he would have to face the bathrooms.

That's where he was when Sara and James came through the gate into the backyard. The little kids. Sara, at age nine, was the kind of girl who stars in Christmas programs at the elementary school: long, blond hair; a photogenic face; intelligent and witty, with a flair for the dramatic; on the run from dawn to dark. That was Sara.

With Sara was her little brother James, or, as he was affectionately known in the family, Jamie. At three years and two months, the little boy was the antithesis of his sister: quiet; shy; distant. The one thing they had in common was good looks. Jamie's most prominent feature was his brown, curly hair. He had lots of it, and it was striking. Below the hair was a little boy's face, dotted with freckles on the cheeks and forehead. Jamie's body was tall and wiry, sturdy for his age. People said he resembled his father and would probably look just like him when he grew up.

Right now Jamie's appearance was accented by an unusual patch of color in his hair. Brian blinked and looked again. Then he perceived the source of the bright color. Jamie was wearing a flower in his hair. Well, not exactly a flower, he decided. A dandelion. The small yellow weed had been carefully placed right on top of his head with the stem poking into his hair so it wouldn't fall off. Like a gargoyle, the unusual decoration was at once unsightly and beautiful. The boy seemed oblivious to its presence, a fact which only highlighted the strangeness of the blossom's appearance.

"Hi, daddy. Jamie and I have been out for a walk. I put the pretty flower in his hair. Don't you think he looks pretty?" Sara turned to admire her little brother's hair and giggled happily.

"Well, yeah. I guess he does look kind of cute," answered her father. "I'm not sure you picked the best flower around, but it does brighten up his face a little." Brian bent down to get a better look. "How do you like the flower in your hair, Jamie?" he asked with a chuckle in his voice.

Jamie wasn't paying attention to either his father or the flower. He was watching a cat that had just climbed over the fence into the backyard.

Brian turned back to Sara. "Been having fun, then?" he asked.

"Oh, yes, daddy! It's such a nice day, don't you think? I just took Jamie and we went over to the park and I pushed him on the swings for a while. He loves to go on the swings. That's where I found Jamie's flower. I picked it and gave it to him. He seemed to like it so I put it in his hair. And we saw some other kids there and they were playing tag. We just watched them for a while and then we came home."

"Well, sounds like you had fun. Next time you go to the park, remember to ask first, okay?"

"Okay, daddy."

And with that, Sara turned and ran into the house, beckoned by some new adventure. Brian watched her go and shook his head. How was a father supposed to keep up with someone like her? But he smiled at the thought.

He turned back to his son. Lifting the little boy and holding him in his right arm, he took the shovel in his other hand and walked slowly back into the garage. After returning the shovel, he went back into the kitchen. He stooped and gently put Jamie down on his feet. Then he plucked the dandelion flower from the boy's hair and patted him gently on the behind. He watched as Jamie shuffled slowly out of the kitchen and down the hallway.

Brian took another look at the dandelion. How like Sara to turn a weed into a flower. And how like her to dress up her little brother. Sara's fondness for Jamie had surfaced before. She loved to play with him, talk to him, wait on him. He was her little personal doll. And even if the relationship was kind of one-sided, it seemed genuine.

Brian was still fingering the dandelion as he walked into the living room and discovered Marianne dusting the piano. He wondered if that was her job or if *she* had traded with someone, too. Marianne was considerably shorter than her husband, with coal black hair and a dark olive complexion. While not a stunning woman, after sixteen years of marriage she still possessed the face and figure that had attracted Brian to her.

Like her husband, Marianne was partial to the humanities; her specialties were music and drama. She had spent countless hours learning to play the cello, and the beautiful instrument in the big black case in her bedroom was one of her prized possessions. She also played the piano and had a fair singing voice. She had been in the drama club in high school, landing major parts in four different plays during her junior and senior years. Brian viewed Marianne's artistic accomplishments with genuine admiration. She set the family standard for sensitivity and culture.

Marianne spied the dandelion in Brian's hand. "What have you got there, hon?" she asked, and then, before he could respond, continued teasingly: "I know you're having fun in the yard, but you really don't need to bring your weeds into the house. We've got enough dirt in here already."

Brian laughed and held the rapidly wilting flower out for his wife to inspect. "Bad guess," he said. "I didn't get this from the yard. As a matter of fact, Sara brought it home from the park. In Jamie's hair."

"In Jamie's hair?"

"Yup. She thought it made him look cute. And it did kind of make him look cute. But what was funny was watching the two of them. Can you picture it? Sara is getting all excited about taking her little brother to the park, planting a flower in his hair. And Jamie? Well, he could care less about what's going on. Sara could put grasshoppers in his hair for all he cares." Brian laughed again.

Marianne cut the laugh short. "So what did Jamie do?" she inquired with more than curiosity in her voice. "I mean, did he seem to be having fun? Do you think he enjoyed going to the park with his sister?"

"Well, I think so. Sara said he really liked the swings." Brian stopped talking for a moment. The look on Marianne's face made him dig a little deeper. "You know," he continued, "It's hard to tell with him. He doesn't seem to get too excited about things. Just not quite like his sister." His voice trailed off as he looked again at his wife. "Hey, Marianne, why are you looking so serious all of a sudden? It really wasn't a big deal. They just went over to the park and back. I know you don't like Sara going places alone, but . . ."

Marianne interrupted again. "It's not that. I'm not worried about the dandelion, or even about Sara going to the park. It's just a couple of blocks away and we're in a good neighborhood. No, that's not what I'm thinking about. But your little story reminded me of something I've been wanting to talk to you about," she continued, taking Brian by the hand and leading him across the room as she spoke. They sat down at opposite ends of the couch, turning sideways so they could face each other. Marianne hesitated for a moment—perhaps to organize her thoughts—then got to the point. "I think there's something wrong with Jamie," she said in slow, measured syllables. She paused again. Brian opened his mouth to ask a question, but she stilled him with a finger to her lips. "Brian, the older Jamie gets, the more concerned I get about him. Something is wrong with his development."

Brian took a deep breath and let it out all at once. "Something wrong with his development?" he echoed. "You mean because he's not talking very much, yet? Is that what you're worried about?"

She nodded her head. "That's part of it."

Brian didn't know whether to agree or disagree. So he thought for a moment. before he spoke. Then he continued: "Yeah, I know what you mean. He should be talking more by now. I think about it sometimes, too." He got up from his position at the end of the couch and moved closer to Marianne. "You know," he added, "We talked about this once before. Do you remember?" Marianne nodded affirmatively, so he continued: "Didn't we decide that maybe we were being overly concerned? Lots of kids don't learn to talk until they're a little older, especially the ones with quiet personalities. Jamie's barely three years old. Maybe he just needs more time."

"No, Brian. There's more to it than that. I used to be content just to wait and watch. But not anymore. I don't know what it is or even how I know, but something is seriously wrong with our son."

This time he didn't say anything. This whole discussion had caught him unprepared and he didn't know whether to side with Marianne or try to represent a more impartial view of the issue. He had learned one thing over the years, however: when Marianne was this intense he had better take her seriously. So he sat back and listened. But even then he wasn't quite prepared for what came next.

"I think Jamie has some kind of developmental disorder," Marianne continued. "And I don't think his mind functions normally."

That got a reaction. "Marianne, you're making a pretty big assumption to say something like that." He shook his head, then turned and looked into her face. "He's just a little boy. How could you possibly think he's . . . not normal?"

She toppled back into the cushion and drew her legs up against her body, clutching them tightly with both arms. "You remember last month when I took Jamie to get his picture taken? Well, something happened down there. I was watching the other children—what they did, how they were acting, how they reacted to the photographer. Most of them were much younger than Jamie. Then when I put Jamie up there to get his picture taken, the contrast was so dramatic. It wasn't just that he didn't say anything. It was the way he acted. It was all the things he *didn't* do. He was a stick figure up there. No life. No form. It was like he was totally clueless that anything was going on. I don't know how to describe it, but I could see it so clearly. I just realized all of a sudden that he was . . . well, different."

Marianne sat up. She put her hand on Brian's back and rubbed gently between his shoulders as she spoke. "Brian, he's not a normal child."

Once again he didn't respond. But this time it was because he just didn't know what to say.

◆◆◆

Jamie didn't look any different than any other three-year-old kid. At least, that's the way Brian saw it as he watched his son from a distance. In all the hours he had spent with Jamie, he had never studied him like this. He felt uncomfortable judging his own son's every movement and action as though he were a subject in a social science experiment. But today Brian was a researcher, not a father.

Jamie was sitting on the carpet in the corner of his room. On the floor in front of him were a couple of toys—a Fisher Price record player that played what Sara called the "bumpy records," and a bright red fire truck with silver ladders on the sides. Right now Jamie wasn't listening to the record player and he wasn't playing with the fire truck. He was playing with a pencil. He had grasped the pencil firmly with his right hand. From time to time he would hold it up close to his eyes and study it intently or wave it around in front of his face. Then he would drop his hand to his side. After a few seconds he would raise the pencil up in front of his face again. He seemed to be fascinated by the bright yellow stick.

Nothing unusual about this, Brian thought to himself. What he saw was a little boy who had found a simple toy. He checked his watch as he continued to monitor Jamie's activities. Five minutes went by. Ten minutes. Jamie continued to play with the pencil, following the same pattern over and over. Brian frowned. It seemed like a long time for a child to keep doing the same thing without some kind of change or interruption.

He moved a little closer to his son and studied him more intently. Jamie was wearing a blue T-shirt with the words *Little All-Star* on the front, a pair of red shorts, yellow socks, and black sneakers—the kind with Velcro fasteners.

Brian reminded himself that Jamie was a good-looking kid. He would probably be quite handsome when he graduated from high school.

If he graduated from high school.

Brian caught himself. *I'm getting as jumpy as my wife,* he thought. He tried to step back and look at the whole thing objectively. What concrete evidence did they have that this little boy had some kind of serious developmental disorder?

Nothing, really. Still, he had to agree that Jamie was unusually reserved and introverted. And then there was that strange behavior with the pencil . . .

Brian stood up and moved over by his son. Lifting the little boy in his arms, he bent down and spoke directly into the tiny ear. "Hi, Jamie. How's Daddy's special little guy doing today? You having fun with your fire truck?"

Jamie waved his pencil.

Brian pointed. "There, Jamie. There's your fire truck. And it's a good-looking one. Can you say 'fire truck'?"

Jamie waved the pencil again.

Placing the little boy carefully on the floor, Brian walked over to the fire truck and picked it up. He sat down in front of his son, gently removed the pencil from the boy's hand, and put the pencil on the floor.

"Here's your fire truck, Jamie. Look. Isn't this a neat one? See how big it is? Look at those wheels. And the ladders. Would you like to play with this?" Brian held out the fire truck. He lifted up Jamie's arms and tucked the big red truck between the little hands.

For an instant, Jamie stood there with the fire truck in his arms. Then he sat down abruptly. The big toy tumbled to the floor. Retrieving the pencil, Jamie lifted it up and began waving it rhythmically from side to side.

Brian walked slowly out of the room. He tried to analyze this experience. What did it mean? What had he learned?

Not very much. Enough, however, to make him wonder. Enough to suspect that a relationship he had taken for granted was far shallower than he had supposed. Enough to realize that he didn't know very much about his own son.

Jamie was a closed book to him.

Chapter Two
November 1983

"James Robert Spencer."

Marianne looked up at the nurse standing in the open doorway. Hurriedly, she closed the copy of *Newsweek* she had been reading and tossed it on top of the other magazines loosely scattered on the mahogany end table. *Well, I've learned one thing,* she mused. The magazines in a neurologist's office are the same as the magazines in every other doctor's office.

Glancing at Brian, she took Jamie by the hand and followed the nurse down the corridor to an examination room. Accustomed to waiting with Jamie in a pediatrician's office, Marianne couldn't help but notice how this room was different. No bead-threaders. No building blocks. No picture books. The wallpaper had circles and triangles instead of cakes and clowns. And there were no kiddy chairs. Just the customary sink, cupboards, and an examination table covered with white paper. It looked very serious. Marianne took a deep breath and tried to ease the pounding in her chest.

When the door opened fifteen minutes later, a small, stocky man with thinning hair entered the room. He looked pretty serious, too. "Hello. I'm Doctor Morrison," he advised in a deep voice that, if not over-friendly, was not unkind either. He opened the folder that he had taken from the slot on the door as he entered the room and scanned quickly through the papers inside. "Let's see. You're Mr. and Mrs. Spencer."

"And this is James," said Marianne as she walked over to where Jamie was standing in the middle of the floor. She lifted him up to face the doctor. Doctor Morrison looked Jamie in the eye—or tried to. The little boy squirmed and turned his head. The doctor reached out and took Jamie's chin in his hands, holding the little head still. "Hello, James," he said. He studied the face for a moment and looked searchingly into the boy's eyes. Jamie squealed and fought to get free.

Releasing his grip on Jamie, Doctor Morrison turned to Marianne again. "I have the results of the tests that were done at the hospital last week. Looks like we did a CT scan and an EEG. Nothing unusual. Both tests were normal. Which doesn't necessarily mean that everything *is* normal, of course. You obviously suspect some kind of problem or you wouldn't be here. Why don't you tell me what it is that you're concerned about. What kind of symptoms have you seen?"

Marianne and Brian exchanged glances. Seeing the go-ahead look in her husband's eyes, Marianne said, "Well, I guess the main thing is that he doesn't talk. He's over three and a half years old now and he only knows a few words. You know, he can say things like 'drink' and 'no' and a few other words, but that's about it. He doesn't seem to understand or listen to what we say to him either. And he does some strange things, like getting obsessed with certain toys and objects. It just seems like maybe his brain isn't working right or something."

"When did you first notice that something was wrong?"

"It's been during the last year or so. The first two years of his life seemed pretty normal. I guess it's been mostly in the last few months that we've really become concerned. I talked to Dr. Charney—he's our pediatrician—about it when we had Jamie in for a check-up a couple of months ago. He agreed that Jamie should be checked by a specialist and referred us to you."

"Okay. Thank you." Dr. Morrison glanced at his clipboard. "Has James been involved in any accidents? Any injury to the head that you can think of?"

"Not really."

Brian spoke up. "The only thing that's been at all unusual was his birth. He was very large, almost ten pounds, and Marianne had a tough delivery. It took a long time to get him delivered. When he was finally born, his color wasn't good. Kind of a bluish tint. The color got better quick, though. We had him checked right away by a pediatrician. He said everything was okay."

"There was something else unusual about his development," Marianne volunteered. "Now that I think about it, Jamie has been sick a lot. Ever since he was a tiny baby. Sore throats, ear infections, runny nose, cough. You name it. Seems like he was on antibiotics half the time when he was a little baby. It's been a little better lately, but he still gets sick a lot." Marianne turned to look at her husband. "Is there anything else we're overlooking, Brian?" she asked. He shook his head. "I guess that's about it, then," she concluded.

During this conversation, the neurologist had been meticulously scribbling notes on a log in his folder. Now he put down his clipboard and stood up. "Let's have a closer look at James. Would you please take off his clothes and put him on the table?"

Marianne took Jamie by the hand and pulled him toward the examination table. She could feel tension in the little body. As she pulled off his shirt, he began screaming and kicking. Marianne gritted her teeth and reached for a shoe . . .

✦✦✦

Dusk was settling over Colorado Springs when they got back to the car. Marianne paused to allow Brian to open the car door for her and Jamie. She climbed inside, pulling the little boy after her. With her knees facing backward, she lifted him over the top of the front seat and secured him in his car seat while Brian walked around to the driver's side of the car and got in behind the wheel.

The parking lot was bordered on one side by the medical building and on the other side by a hill that sloped gradually down into the valley below. From their vantage point they could see over the edge of the hill. Lights were starting to blink on in the city below. A flock of starlings swarmed by just above the crest of the hill where a handful of trees jutted out from the otherwise barren hillside.

Marianne sat motionlessly in the car, head bowed, eyes staring at the carpet by her feet. She didn't speak, even though Brian made no attempt to start the car. She felt uncomfortable, wished that he would say something or do something. Was he waiting for her to talk? Well, she didn't feel like talking.

Each second seemed an hour. Brian sat there behind the wheel, rigid as a post, staring through the window at the lights in the city below. Finally she could stand it no longer. And when she started to talk there was more than a touch of harshness in her voice.

"Well, I guess we know now, don't we?"

Brian did not respond. Again she suffered through the silence that hung like a dark cloud around her.

Then she started to cry. Words and tears flowed out together in one big gush. "Oh, Brian," she wailed, "How could he say in one breath that the tests were normal, then turn around and say that Jamie had multiple disabilities and his life would not be normal? All in that cold matter-of-fact voice of his. And after all that he still didn't tell us exactly what the problem is or what can be done about it. We don't know any more now than we did before!"

Brian touched his wife's knee reassuringly. "We do know more than we did, Marianne. We know there's a problem. That's worth something."

"Sure it is," she retorted bitterly. "A lot of good that does!"

Brian leaned back against the car door. His fingers toyed with the keys dangling from the ignition. He seemed to be groping for words. "I know it's hard now, Marianne," he said finally. "I feel terrible about this whole thing—just like you. Let's not try to figure it all out tonight. Okay? We'll keep working on it. We'll find a way to deal with it." He put his arm around Marianne and pulled her close for a moment. She was crying freely now.

He sat silently for a few more seconds, then slowly fastened his seat belt and started the engine. Maneuvering carefully through the parking lot, he pulled out onto the street and followed it down the side of the hill. Marianne was sobbing quietly. She thought of the little boy in the back seat, wondered what he was doing, wondered what he was feeling, wondered if he knew that he was abnormal. Most of all, she wondered what was wrong with him and what would happen to him. She turned to look at him. Jamie was staring out the car window, watching the moving trees and bushes at the side of the road. For once his silence matched his companions.

They were downtown now. The short winter evening had transformed quickly into night. Brian turned to Marianne. "Want to stop and get something to eat? Why don't we pick up something so we won't have to make dinner tonight?"

Marianne managed a weak smile. She nodded her head, grateful for the change of subject.

Brian turned into a Burger King and pulled into the line for the drive-through window.

◆◆◆

Marianne was confused. Although she believed Dr. Morrison when he said that something was wrong with Jamie, she had already known that; he had convinced her husband, but merely confirmed her own fears without telling her anything new. So what *was* wrong with Jamie? *I've had three children,* she told herself, *and two of them are perfectly fine; the problem is not with me. Or with Brian.* Guilt was the last thing she needed right now, but she discovered that questions about her own self-adequacy had a way of returning so that she must deal with them over and over.

On her lunch break from the real estate office, and after dropping off a client following a house visit, she prowled the library, finding sections she had never run across in her college years, learning to read medical indexes, getting comfortable with terms she seldom ran across in daily life. She learned she was not alone, that there were other Jamies out there, and some of them were worse off than her son. Jamie could be at home with her, he could sit at the table and eat, he could play with his toys. Many disabled children were denied even those simple functions. But this was small consolation; she still had no clear idea about the nature of the problem or what to do about it.

Then she had a breakthrough. The idea first came into her mind while she was walking and thinking in the little park down the street from her house. She wasn't sure she was even thinking about Jamie when she made the important connection.

Language. The problem had something to do with language, with talking. She had known that all along, of course, but somehow she had never recognized it as an avenue to a solution. Her research efforts had focused primarily on medical conditions and behavioral problems. Now she realized that Jamie's inability to communicate was a major feature — a key to understanding his limitation. Marianne hurried back to the library and searched out a book on speech development in children. She scanned the book quickly right there in the library stacks. It took only a moment to affirm that Jamie's language development was way behind other children of his age. She felt that she was on to something, but she still had no name for Jamie's condition. *I need more help,* she realized. Professional help. Should she go back to the doctors, try another specialist? *No,* she talked herself out of that one. So what other help was available?

Then she thought of Uncle Curtis.

Curtis Noble. Her mother's brother. She had been to his home in Boulder several times. She had never thought much about his profession before: Uncle Curtis was a speech pathologist at the University of Colorado. Perhaps he could help. The next day Marianne phoned him and arranged to see him the following week.

That phone call cheered her up considerably. She learned that help was available for children with speech disorders. Maybe all Jamie needed was some extra help from a speech therapist. Tutor the little guy for a couple of years and he just might catch up with his peers. She would marshal whatever resources were required to do the job.

Uncle Curtis had insisted that Marianne come for dinner. "It's been years since I've seen you, Marianne. Or your family. I want all of you to come and have dinner with Helen and me."

Angela begged off in favor of a birthday party at a friend's house. That left Marianne, Brian, Sara, and Jamie to fulfill the dinner invitation. When they arrived at Curtis Noble's home, he greeted them warmly and ushered them right into the dining room. A distinguished gray-haired man in his late fifties, Marianne's uncle exuded both a relaxed attitude and a professional assurance that generated instant confidence. Seeing him again fueled Marianne's hopes and eased some of her recurring apprehensions about this visit.

Curtis and his wife lived alone in an elegant two-story home. They had two children—both long since gone—and seemed happy to have company on an otherwise dark and cold winter evening. The dinner conversation was comfortably casual. How old were each of Marianne and Brian's children? Was Sara still taking violin lessons and developing that special talent of hers? How did Brian like his job at Palmer High School? How was Marianne's mother feeling since her recent surgery? The Nobles were congenial hosts and the roast, smothered in potatoes and vegetables, was succulent.

During the meal Jamie sat in a tall oak chair, his small brown eyes barely level with the top of the table. He ate heartily, almost greedily; his eating habits had always been inversely correlated with his communication skills. There was a distraction—Sara kept poking him and giggling at him while he was trying to eat—but he pushed her hands aside with more than a little annoyance so he could concentrate on his dinner. Jamie's great-uncle had glanced at him from time to time during the meal. Now the older man turned his attention directly to the child and spoke to him.

"Well, Jamie," he said. "Did you like the food?"

Jamie sat quietly, his eyes fixed on the ceiling fan that he had just discovered whirring above his head. The fan's movements were so deliberate and predictable. The boy was both fascinated and soothed by the whirling blades. If he heard the question from his great-uncle at all, he paid no attention to it.

Curtis was watching Jamie now, tracking his movements just as carefully as the boy traced the motions of the fan. After a few moments he made another attempt to communicate. "How old are you, Jamie? This many?" He held up three fingers and pointed to them with his other hand.

No response. The boy was as still as the figures on the tablecloth. His perfect record of silence since entering the Noble residence remained intact.

Curtis arose from his position on the other side of the table and walked around to where Marianne and Brian were sitting. "Would you mind if I just, uh, talk with him for a few minutes?" he asked. Marianne nodded consent. Then Curtis walked over to Jamie's chair and knelt down beside him. He placed one hand on the boy's shoulder. Jamie pulled away at the man's touch but did not look at him. He appeared to be trying to ignore him.

"Jamie," the professor said slowly and soothingly. "Jamie, I want to talk to you for a few minutes. Will you come and sit by me?" He took the boy gently by the arm and lifted him down from his chair. Jamie squirmed, but did not try to run away. Shuffling his feet awkwardly, he allowed Uncle Curtis to guide him across the room to a sofa. The older man sat down and lifted Jamie up beside him.

From her vantage point across the room, Marianne watched what was happening as if she were a spectator in a courtroom. She could feel blood pulsing through her chest and noticed that she was feeling light-headed and giddy. She was counting heavily on this evaluation and hoped desperately that the results would not be disappointing. *I'll even take bad news*, she said to herself. *Just don't leave me hanging with nothing.*

Marianne couldn't hear any of the conversation between the man and the boy, which made visual and nonverbal actions that much more obvious. While the boy's face betrayed uncertainty and anxiety, his little body hardly moved. Uncle Curtis was talking to him, but he wasn't answering. The professor tried talking close to the boy's ear. No response. He gently turned Jamie's face toward him and spoke to him again. Still no response. He tried using his hands, making motions that Marianne recognized as sign language, though she didn't understand them. Curtis pointed to Jamie's parents across the room, to the table, even to the ceiling fan that was still circling overhead. Jamie was a statue. Marianne could detect no reaction whatever to anything Uncle Curtis did.

He's facing this situation by pretending it doesn't exist, Marianne realized suddenly. She began to wonder if Jamie just didn't like people. Maybe that was why he didn't talk. Maybe . . .

Reminding herself that wild hypothesizing would take her nowhere, Marianne tried to refocus her eyes and mind on her son and uncle. As far as she could tell, Uncle Curtis had not succeeded in getting Jamie to talk. She turned to her husband and saw that he was talking to Sara. She picked up snatches of their conversation, realized that they were talking about Emily, one of Sara's friends at school. Something about Emily and her family going to California for Christmas. So Brian wasn't really paying attention to the drama on the other side of the room. He seemed to be content to just wait and see how it worked out. Marianne sighed. Sometimes she wished she could be more like her husband and not take life so seriously. But how could she do that when so much was hanging in the balance?

In any case, the interview seemed to be over. Uncle Curtis was walking back across the room, holding Jamie's hand and leading him carefully back to his parents. "Well," he said, "Jamie and I have had a little talk." He paused and looked first at Marianne, then at Brian. Marianne heard the soft purring sound of the ceiling fan once again as she waited impatiently for him to continue.

"It's hard to figure out exactly what's going on in such a short time," he went on. He smiled. "As you know, he doesn't talk very much."

Another pause. This time Curtis hesitated as if he didn't know exactly what to say. "However, I suspect that Jamie has some kind of significant communication disorder. It's more than just a personality trait or even a speech impediment."

Marianne's heart sank. This was not what she had hoped to hear. But her need to know pressed her to find out more. "Do you have any idea what it might be, Uncle Curtis?" Even as she asked the question, Marianne knew by the look on her uncle's face that she wasn't going to get a clear answer.

"I'm sorry, Marianne. I'm afraid Jamie's condition is outside my area of expertise. I have some ideas about what could be wrong, but anything I would say would just be speculation."

Marianne's heart sank again. Another disappointment. Still no answers. As if listening from a great distance, she heard Uncle Curtis conclude his explanation.

"However, I would like to send you to one of my colleagues. His name is Gerald Haslam. He's a psychologist at the university; specializes in communicative disorders. I think he may be able to give you a more specific diagnosis. I'd be happy to contact him and set up an appointment for you. Would you like me to do that?"

Marianne's mind was straying again, racing down shadowy mental pathways that inevitably lead to dead ends. Suddenly she was very tired. She heard herself saying, almost as if the voice came from someone else . . .

"Yes, of course. We'd be very grateful if you would do that."

◆◆◆

Brian turned the lock and opened the front door of the house. Marianne slipped quietly past him, stumbled into the living room and collapsed wearily on the couch. He followed her into the room and sat down on the carpet at her feet.

Marianne reached up and turned on the table lamp. Slowly, methodically, she unfolded the paper that had been clutched in her left hand. Carefully smoothing out the creases, she focused on the last two paragraphs and read them for the third time.

> This three-year, nine-month-old boy shows a number of indicators of early infantile autism. Although estimated intellectual function would place him in a retarded range, observational inferences suggest that he has normal motor development and memory. He shows evidence of several behavioral deficiencies often noted in autism. His play behavior is generally non-specific and idiosyncratic. He has developed no friendships and does not interact with children in any adaptive way. There are almost no attachments to family, although he does not totally resist their interactions. He shows marked attention deficit and little or no eye-to-eye contact. There is almost no evidence of language development although speech sounds have developed.
>
> All evidences taken together suggest an autistic pattern and this child might benefit more from a treatment program geared to these symptoms rather than a typical program for mental retardation. He is not currently showing marked behavior problems and in this regard shows a much better prognosis than many children with this disorder.
>
> DIAGNOSTIC IMPRESSION: Infantile Autism, full syndrome present
>
> Gerald D. Haslam, Ph.D.
> Consulting Clinical Psychologist

She folded the paper again, and dropped the hand that was holding it into her lap. Suddenly she began to cry. Held in check for almost an hour by monumental effort, the tears broke loose with the crash of a summer thunderstorm. She sobbed uncontrollably for several minutes. Brian moved up beside her, put his arms around her and held her close for a long time. "Marianne," he whispered hoarsely, stroking her hair and kissing her face repeatedly.

When she could speak, she called his name and hung on it for support. "Oh, Brian," she cried. "Not this. I never thought it would be anything like this. *Autism*! Not Jamie. Not our son."

He looked into her face. "Marianne, listen to me. It's just a word. There are lots of children who have this condition."

"Brian, I'm afraid. Everything I've ever heard about autism is so awful. Children who never talk. They just sit and rock all day. They stay up all night. They don't ever look at people. They . . . hurt themselves." Her sobbing reached a new crescendo. "I can't stand the thought of Jamie being like that!"

"Marianne, let's not cross bridges that aren't there yet. The psychologist said his condition isn't as severe as many autistic children. Remember? Maybe he'll do better than we think. At least now we have some idea what's wrong. We can finally do something to help him."

She didn't answer. Shaking her head, she pulled his arms away and turned her back to him. Then she got up from the couch and walked out of the room and down the hallway to the master bedroom. Brian gave a deep sigh and fell back into the cushions of the couch.

Marianne closed the bedroom door behind her. With reflexive movements that seemed more like a dream than reality, she undressed and put on her nightgown. Only after she had put her clothes away and sat down on the edge of the bed did she try to face her thoughts. The despair that had swirled nebulously through her mind for weeks had finally taken a definite and terrifying shape. So now she knew. The wait was over, the mystery solved, the answer found. But the questions were just beginning. What was ahead for Jamie? For her and Brian and the girls? Would she be trapped at home caring for a disabled child? Would Jamie remain totally non-communicative? Would he ever be able to dress himself and bathe himself? Would he go to school? Would he end up in an institution someday? Her mind jumped precipitously from one dreadful scenario to another.

Unexpectedly, her thoughts settled upon another unbidden image: Brian sitting dejectedly on the couch where she had left him. A wave of guilt washed over her. She hadn't meant to leave him like that, didn't want to hurt him just because she was hurting. But this was one of those times when she just had to be alone. She hoped he would understand.

Marianne forced her attention back to her surroundings. Absently she pulled back the covers, turned off the light, and got into bed. She lay there for a long time, praying for insensibility. The tears had stopped, but deep down inside the part of her that was a mother ached and wept for the loss of ever so many hopes and dreams.

Finally, mercifully, she fell asleep.

Chapter Three
December 1983

Thanks to a late afternoon faculty meeting at school, it was well past 5:00 when Brian got home from work. The first thing he saw—still half a block away—was the string of colored Christmas lights along the top ridge of the house. The lights triggered a brief moment of nostalgia, a longing for other Christmases when life had been a little brighter.

Two or three inches of new snow had fallen on the driveway during the day. As the little front-wheel drive Sentra crunched hungrily into the unbroken crust on the left side of the driveway, Brian noticed the parallel tracks from the van at the right. So Marianne was home already. It didn't always work out that way; sometimes he arrived first. But tonight he was glad that she was already home. He looked forward to seeing her, even if the reception might not be up to past standards. For more than two weeks now, their interactions had been colder than December nights in Colorado Springs, and he was hungry for some understanding and affection. Well, tonight they had a date. Maybe something good would happen.

Once he was inside the garage, Brian snatched his briefcase from the back seat, climbed out of the car and opened the door into the kitchen. Marianne was just putting the finishing touches on dinner. Brian noticed right away that she was already dressed for the concert. She was wearing a navy blue dress, mid-calf length with white ruffles around the neckline, white hose, and stylish black shoes. Very pretty, he thought to himself. Pretty enough to be a display in a department store window. The problem was, right now he felt like he was outside the window looking in.

Angela was assigned to help with dinner tonight. In addition to helping her mother, she was talking to one of her friends on the telephone. In the battle for her attention, the telephone was clearly ahead of dinner.

Easing his way past the walking telephone, Brian went to his wife and put his arms around her. Marianne gave him a quick hug, then shifted her attention back to her electric frying pan, where half a dozen hamburgers sizzled. Seizing a spatula, she turned the steaming patties over and sprinkled on some seasoning salt. "Angie, would you please finish setting the table?" she called out as she continued to doctor the meat. "How was school today?" she asked Brian, looking over her shoulder to see if Angela had responded to her request.

"Okay, I guess. How about you? Anything exciting happen at the office today?"

"Well, I sold a house."

Brian waited for more details, but Marianne's attention seemed to be elsewhere. At the moment she was checking the French fries in the oven to see if they were done. "Just a sec, honey," she apologized, turning her head to look for her daughter. Angela had disappeared from the room, but the telephone cord that was stretched around the corner into the hallway was a dead giveaway to her whereabouts.

"Angie, did you hear what I said about finishing the table?" Marianne called out. She began scraping the French fries off the cookie sheet with the spatula, scooping them into a large metal bowl. She was busy with her kitchen tasks, and further conversation would have to wait. Brian sighed. Lots of things seemed to have been put on hold lately.

In any case, it was almost time for dinner. Angela was finally off the telephone and had begun setting the plates and silverware around the table. Brian snagged his briefcase from where he had left it in the middle of the floor and took it into the bedroom. He went into the bathroom and washed his hands. Then he returned to the kitchen and sat down at the table. Jamie was already there, sitting in his usual spot and waiting patiently for dinner. Jamie was always on time for dinner.

Sara appeared momentarily. She danced into the room and hopped onto a chair. "What's for dinner, mom?" she asked as she peered over the top of the counter.

"Hamburgers and fries," replied Marianne, trying to respond to the familiar question as if hearing it for the first time. To prove her point, she picked up the plate of hamburgers and bowl of fries and plopped them down in the center of the table.

Soon everyone was seated at the table. As family members began filling their plates with food, Marianne took advantage of her proximity to Angela to do some checking up. "Angie, did you remember that you're baby-sitting for us tonight?" she asked.

"Yes, mom," Angela replied, her voice almost inert with enthusiasm. "Actually," she added more hopefully, "Stephanie invited me to go to a movie with her and Karen. Is there any way I could go? Maybe I could baby-sit tomorrow night instead?"

"I'm sorry, Angie. Dad and I have plans for this evening and we need you to watch Sara and Jamie. You can go to the movie another time. Okay?"

"Yes, mom," she repeated. This time there was no postscript.

Marianne flashed a brief smile of appreciation at Angela. Then she turned her attention to the items on her plate. For a time, everyone ate quietly. Between bites of his hamburger, Brian glanced around the table. Angela was still trying to put her hamburger together and seemed to be having problems with the ketchup bottle. Sara was poking at her French fries, which was the only thing on her plate. He looked at Jamie. The little boy was leaning forward in his booster chair, capturing his food with his fingers and gulping it down. Brian marveled at his son's appetite. Jamie probably ate more than both of his older sisters combined. Definitely.

Sara made a move to get up from the table. However, her untouched plate had not gone unnoticed. Marianne stopped her before she could get away. "Sara? Aren't you going to eat anything?" she asked.

"I don't like any of this stuff, mom," the girl answered. "Besides, I'm just not very hungry tonight, I guess."

"Are you sure you wouldn't like a hamburger? Or you could get something out of the refrigerator. There's some leftover spaghetti from last night if you want that."

"Well, could I maybe just have some ice cream or something like that?" Sara was treading on tenuous ground with this request, but she apparently thought it was worth a try.

"Not until you eat something else," was the firm reply.

"I don't want anything else. Ice cream is the only thing that sounds good right now."

"Sorry. No dinner, no ice cream."

"Well, I guess I'll have some spaghetti, then." Sara dragged herself out of the chair and worked her way over to the refrigerator. She opened the door, fished out the Tupperware container with spaghetti in it, dished up a couple of spoonfuls, and put the plate into the microwave oven.

By this time Angela had disappeared from the kitchen, and Jamie had wandered off as well. Brian began the clean-up. Putting the eating utensils aside, he collected all of the loose plates from around the table, leaving only Sara's setting intact. He methodically stacked the glasses until he had made a little tower. Picking up the plates and glasses, he walked over to the sink and started rinsing them off and placing them one by one into the dishwasher. Marianne joined him, opening a cupboard to put away the salt and pepper.

Out of the corner of his eye, Brian saw Jamie come back into the kitchen. He was carrying something in his right hand— a small, shiny object. When Jamie held the object up to admire it and Brian realized what it was, he moved quickly to intercept.

"No, Jamie," he said quietly but firmly. "That's daddy's special watch. You can't play with it." Gently he pried the gold timepiece out of the boy's hands. "Come on, let's see if we can find your car for you."

Taking Jamie by the hand, Brian led him along the hallway and into the master bedroom. The little toy car that Jamie had been carrying around for days was on the carpet, right by the desk where he had apparently dropped it in exchange for the gold pocket watch — the ancient watch that had been owned by Brian's father and grandfather. Brian picked up the car and put it back into the little boy's hand. Then he scooted Jamie out the door.

He turned to the watch in his hand and checked it carefully to make sure it was okay. Nothing was damaged. The shiny instrument was as beautiful and mysterious as ever. And just as silent, the hands locked in their timeless position of twenty-seven minutes past twelve.

Brian liked the old pocket watch. Somehow, holding it and thinking about it made him feel close to his family. Seventy-five years ago the watch had been beautiful and useful. It was still beautiful, but no longer able to perform the function for which it was created. What had the jeweler said? That it couldn't be fixed. Other watches and clocks ticked and hummed all through the house, but the most exquisite timepiece was silent. It seemed unfair. But no matter. This delicate gold watch was priceless to him, whether it worked or not.

Brian took a tissue from a Kleenex box and carefully wiped off the gold case and the glass face. Then he gently placed the watch back in its accustomed place on his desk. As he left the room, he turned off the light and closed the door behind him.

When he returned to the kitchen, Marianne was finishing loading the dishwasher. Brian crept up silently behind her. He cleared his throat. "It's Friday night," he croaked. "Are mom and dad doing anything exciting tonight?"

"Not unless dad gets on the stick and gets ready to go," was the reply. It sounded a little too businesslike to suit Brian, but he shrugged it off. "As a matter of fact, I was just about ready to go change," he countered. "Let's see. It's 6:30. We need to leave about 7:00, right? Still plenty of time." Brian fished a dish cloth out of the sink and began wiping off the table. The kitchen was almost clean now. "Tell me again about the concert. Who is it we're going to see tonight?"

"Philippe Entremont. He's a pianist, from France. And he's very good. I've got a couple of his albums. Do you remember that record we have of the Grieg Piano Concerto?"

"Yeah, I think so." Classical music wasn't exactly Brian's trump hand, but he had developed a superficial knowledge and modest appreciation for it—largely because of Marianne's acute interest. He thought he could remember the Grieg piece. "Is that what he's playing tonight?" he queried. "The Grieg concerto?"

"No. This thing tonight is a solo recital. No orchestra. I think he's going to play several numbers by Debussy and a Beethoven piano sonata."

Brian tossed the dish cloth back into the sink. "Sounds great," he said. "Whatever he plays, I'm sure I'll enjoy it just being there with the most beautiful woman in the valley." Marianne did not respond right away to the compliment. She was closing the dishwasher. As she fastened the door shut and turned the knob to the on position, Brian reached out and took her hand.

She turned to look at him; for a moment, their eyes met. He couldn't understand everything he saw in her face: worry, disappointment, perhaps some fatigue; but there was also a little more softness than he had seen lately. "Thanks, Brian," she murmured. "Thanks for the compliment. And thanks for coming with me tonight." She gave him a fleeting kiss on the cheek and ushered him out of the room to get ready.

✦✦✦

The pianist's wiry fingers erupted into the opening bars of the *Appassionata* piano sonata. From his position in the darkened concert hall, Brian tried to stay focused on the artist's movements and music—but after a few moments his mind wandered. He had a profound intellectual respect for this music and enjoyed listening to it, but the attraction was not strong enough to capture his undivided attention.

He studied the piano on the stage. It was a grand piano, of course, long and black with lid opened wide and sturdy legs that lifted it above the floor—a wooden ship floating on the darkened stage. He marveled how something so massive could produce the delicate sounds that cascaded over his senses.

Once more he focused on the runs and arpeggios emanating from the big black piano. Philippe Entremont had started to play a cadenza. Brian watched the performer's hands floating effortlessly up and down the keyboard. There was a graceful motion in the movements, as if the physical actions possessed meaning apart from the sounds they produced. The cadenza ended in a crash of emotion and power that sent a little shiver of admiration down Brain's spine.

Not bad, he thought. Maybe if I listened to this stuff a little more often I could really learn to like it.

He looked at Marianne out of the corner of his eye. He could tell that she was really into the music. They were listening to the second movement of the sonata now, a slow, sonorous passage with a simple but haunting theme that recurred in ever more elegant variations. Marianne sat quietly, head bowed, eyes closed. This was familiar, sacred ground for her. For a moment Brian felt jealous of the piano on the stage that owned more of her heart than he did.

The small window of communication that had opened briefly before they left home had closed quickly. The ride to the Fine Arts Center had been awkward, dominated by silence and superficial conversation. He knew why Marianne was so distant, of course. That's why he hadn't pressed too hard. But he was hurting, too.

Brian sighed and burrowed deeper into his seat. He fixed his right knee against the back of the seat in front of him for support. As the Beethoven sonata entered into the third and final movement, he tried once more to focus on the performer and the music. The dark, ominous runs and chords that never quite resolved suited his mood perfectly.

The sonata ended in a thundering display of power and virtuosity. In the *presto* section, the pianist's hands raced daringly up and down the keyboard. His head pitched and swayed under the bright stage lights as he lashed out at the unyielding instrument, exacting every note with flawless precision. Then, abruptly, it was all over. The pianist stood next to the piano bench, bowing repeatedly, one hand resting on the instrument that now acknowledged its conqueror with mute respect. Brian joined in the applause and stood up when everyone else did.

Five minutes later he and Marianne found themselves among the mass of people exiting the Fine Arts Center. Progress up the stairs from the concert hall was painfully slow and it was hot and stuffy in the crowd. Brian was relieved when they finally reached the outside door and felt a draft of cold air on their faces.

Outside a light snow was falling. The lights in the parking lot cast an eerie glow over the snow-covered cars as the tiny flakes danced around them. Brian and Marianne cinched up their coats and lowered their heads to escape the wetness. Holding Marianne's arm, Brian guided her carefully through the snow to the car. When they were both inside and he had brushed the snow off the windshield, Brian started the engine and drove slowly across the parking lot. At the exit he stopped and turned to Marianne. "Want to stop for ice cream?" he suggested.

Startled by the unexpected question, Marianne didn't answer right away. But finally she turned to Brian and nodded her head. He'd been banking on her long-standing love for ice cream to add a little excitement to their evening. In the darkness he couldn't tell if she was genuinely pleased or merely submissive, but right now any kind of *yes* answer was sufficient. So he turned the car downtown and headed for *Melanie's*.

When they entered the ice cream place, they encountered a noisy Friday night crowd. A girl in a pink smock showed them to an empty booth. She wiped off the table and apologized for the mess. "We're pretty busy tonight," she explained. She took their orders and left.

Once again Brian and Marianne found themselves alone together. This time there was no piano to fill in the silence, no snowy drive to divert their attention. Brian tried to start a conversation. "So tell me about the house you sold today," he ventured casually. "Was it that big one you've been trying to sell for six months or however long it's been? You know the one I mean. The six thousand square foot mansion."

Marianne seemed to relax a bit. She leaned back in the booth, allowing her shoulders to sink as she contemplated the question. She smiled at Brian and shook her head slowly, almost teasingly. "No. I'm afraid not. Not that one. It would be nice to sell it, for sure, but no one seems to have a cool three hundred thousand on hand." She met Brian's gaze for a moment, then lowered her eyes to the table. "As a matter of fact," she continued, "The house I sold was a little three-bedroom rambler. The one over on Crescent Drive. I'm afraid the commission won't be quite up to mansion caliber. But it'll help."

"It sure will," echoed Brian. "You know, Marianne, if it wasn't for your real estate work, I don't know how we'd get by—especially at Christmas time. It'd be pretty tough trying to live on my teacher's salary."

"Well, one of these days we may have to live on your teacher's salary," said Marianne under her breath. Brian heard the remark but didn't know what she meant, and she didn't elaborate. He was trying to decide whether to ask for clarification—which would mean facing a now sullen Marianne—when the young girl in the pink smock returned with the ice cream.

"Okay," she asked. "Who had the chocolate shake?"

Brian raised his hand. She put a large glass filled with a thick, creamy liquid on the table in front of him. "And you get the hot caramel sundae," she said to Marianne as she placed the other dish in front of her. The girl put a green slip of paper on the table next to Brian's shake. "Here's the bill," she said. "Just pay at the cash register on your way out."

Brian nodded at the girl as she left. Unwrapping a straw, he made a hole in the milk shake and watched the icy substance fill in the cavity. He tried to remember what they had been talking about, but he couldn't come up with it. Looking at Marianne, he wasn't sure he wanted to talk at all. She didn't look very receptive. So he stuck the straw in his mouth and took a long sip of the milkshake instead.

Marianne picked up her spoon and began eating her sundae. For a time, neither of them spoke. Brian felt his spirits sinking. This date was not going the way he had hoped. The first time they had been together like this since the thing with Jamie, and it was about as romantic as a *Better Homes and Gardens* cookbook. He followed Marianne's lead and stared at the table in front of him, trying to forget for a moment that she was there.

Out of nowhere he heard Marianne's voice.

"I did some Christmas shopping today. Found some things for the girls. And I got a couple of toys for Jamie."

He glanced up and discovered that she was looking at him. She still looked somber, and he couldn't tell if she had spoken because she had something to tell him or because she felt uncomfortable with the silence.

It doesn't matter, he thought. *She's trying.*

He needed to try, too. He opened his mouth to respond to her comment about the Christmas shopping. Then, in mid-thought, he changed his mind.

"Marianne," he said simply. "We need to talk."

She was playing with her spoon, stirring her sundae and watching the topping and ice cream merge into a creamy mixture that was somehow sweeter than either of the original ingredients. His words brought her eyes back up to face him. Her answer was soft, but determined. "Okay, Brian. I think I'm ready. But not here. Let's go home, okay?"

They finished their ice cream in silence. Then Brian helped Marianne to her feet. He paid the bill and led her out of the ice cream place onto the snowy street. His heart was beating fast and his hands felt clammy, which was unusual for him. He told himself he was being irrational to make such a big thing out of this situation. But, the truth was, he felt that part of his life was out of control, that his marriage was falling apart—and it was suddenly very important to him. *I must love her a lot*, he realized as he opened the car door for Marianne and then slid in beside her.

As if everything were on hold, neither of them spoke a word on the way home. Progress was slow on the snow-packed side roads, but at last Brian turned into the driveway and guided the car through the snow into the garage. After the garage door had closed behind them, they sat quietly in the car for a moment, each waiting to see what the other would do. Finally Marianne said, "Shall we go inside?" Without waiting for an answer, she opened the car door, climbed out, and went into the house. Brian followed her in.

Marianne looked quickly around the house, checking to see that Sara and Jamie were in bed and that everything else was okay. She found Angela watching TV in the family room and asked her for a brief report on the evening. Only then did she come into the living room where Brian was waiting. Passing over the vacant spot next to him, she sat down in the recliner.

Brian had hoped that Marianne would start this conversation. But when he saw the tight expression on her face, he realized that he would have to do it. This little discussion was his idea, and she expected him to lead out. How to do it? That was the problem. He decided to lay it out carefully, cover all the bases, and hopefully get some things resolved. "Marianne," he began. "I think you probably know what I'm going to say." He stopped there for a moment to make sure *he* knew what he was going to say, then continued: "The last couple of weeks have been pretty bad for both of us, and I think it's affecting our relationship." He paused again, rubbing the top of his head as he tried to think. He wondered if he was being too analytical. But he had to keep going.

"I know it was tough for you to find out about Jamie," he continued. "It was hard for me, too. But we can't let something like this ruin our lives. It's not fair to us and Angie and Sara. And it's not fair to Jamie, either."

Marianne didn't look any happier after his little speech. He wished he had said it differently, been more discreet. But it was out now, and all he could do was wait for her response.

She didn't answer right away. When she did, the words seemed to have been wrenched from the depths of her soul.

"I know," she whispered hoarsely. Then she began to cry, and when she started there was no stopping it. She wept uncontrollably, and Brian did not interrupt. He sat and watched, helpless before the hurricane he had unleashed.

It was several minutes before Marianne spoke again. She was calmer then—still crying—but the fury was gone.

"Brian," she pleaded. "This has been awfully hard for me. I'm so sorry it's affected our marriage, but . . . I can't help it." She tried to choke back the sobs that threatened to intensify again. "What have we done to deserve something like this? It's so unfair!"

"I know. I feel that way, too," he said simply.

"Then how can you be so cheerful? Honestly, Brian, that's one of the things that bothers me. Sometimes you act as if nothing has happened, like it doesn't matter." There was anger in her voice now.

"Well, maybe I'm not as happy and cheerful as I seem. Maybe that's just my way of coping. I've been trying not to overreact. I'm trying to accept what's happened and go from there. I'm trying to do that," he repeated, "though maybe not as successfully as you think."

When he looked at Marianne again, there was pleading in her eyes. The anger was gone, the wall down. She was a child — vulnerable, defenseless, reaching out for support. Brian got up from the couch and went to her. Taking her by both hands, he lifted her up and pulled her close. For a time they held each other without speaking. Then Brian moved back to the couch and pulled her down beside him.

"Oh, Brian," she murmured, still crying softly. "I'm so sorry. I just don't know what to do." She closed her eyes and leaned back against the cushions. "Brian, what *are* we going to do?"

"I don't know. But we'll do something. We'll find some way to help Jamie. We'll help him to be all he can be. No giving up. Okay?"

He put his arm around her and pulled her head over on his shoulder. She cried some more. Then, gradually her breathing slowed and her body relaxed. For the moment the pain was gone. Brian turned his head and kissed her gently on the forehead.

"Brian, I love you," she whispered as she reached up and rubbed the side of his neck. Then she pulled him close and kissed him tenderly.

This time he was the helpless child. "Marianne," he gasped when he could breathe again. "You haven't kissed me like that for . . . for a long time. Does this mean you're not mad at me any more? Are you feeling better about . . ."

She hushed him with a finger to his lips. "Sometimes you talk too much," she purred. Then she kissed him again.

After that he didn't try to talk any more.

Chapter Four
May 1984

The blue Chevy van maneuvered slowly along the circuitous route of Union Avenue. Marianne drove leisurely, successfully dividing her attention between her driving and her passenger. Unpressured and unhurried, she was enjoying the ride.

"I really appreciate the lift, Marianne," said the other woman. "Sometimes it would be nice to have *two* cars." Looking out the window at the houses on the side of the road, she added: "It would also be great to have a husband to drive the other one. Anyway, like I was saying, thanks for taking me home from the repair shop."

"No problem, Candi. I'm glad for the chance to get out of the house. Since I quit my job, I don't get out as often as I used to. It feels good just to get behind the wheel every now and then, even to run an errand."

Candi Jamison looked about the same age as Marianne, though no one would ever have mistaken them for sisters. Candi was fair-complexioned, with red hair and blue eyes that contrasted markedly with her olive-skinned companion. She and Marianne had been roommates in college. After completing law school, Candi joined a law firm in Colorado Springs. She and Marianne had bumped into each other one day at a local grocery store. Since then they had managed to get together once or twice a year, usually for lunch or some other activity during business hours. Today Marianne was providing backup transportation while Candi had some work done on her car.

Marianne began watching the street signs more carefully. "Let's see, we're getting close to your street, aren't we?"

"It's the next one on the right."

Marianne slowed and swerved into a right turn without stopping. As she straightened the wheel and nudged the car forward again, a loud squawk erupted from the back seat. The initial outburst was followed by prolonged cries of anger and dismay.

"It's just Jamie," Marianne explained apologetically to her passenger. "He's upset because we turned off the main road back there."

"He notices things like that?" Candi looked at Marianne. "Why should it make any difference to him? I thought he was unaware of things going on around him."

"Not really." Marianne smiled at her friend. "True, Jamie doesn't talk a lot, and he doesn't understand everything people say. But he has this uncanny sense of direction. I seriously think he could find his way to any familiar place, even in the dark. We come this way along Union Avenue whenever we go to the grocery store. But usually we just drive along the avenue to the store, then come home the same way. He was expecting me to do that today. When we turned off, he recognized right away that something was different, and that seems to make him nervous. This isn't the first time this has happened. When something disturbs his routine or the way he thinks things should be done, Jamie is very quick to notice it. Amazing, huh?"

"Yes, that is interesting." Candi glanced at the boy in the back seat. She closed her eyes as if she were thinking about something. Then she asked: "Marianne, what exactly is the problem with Jamie? I've never understood exactly what's wrong. I hope you don't mind my asking."

Marianne didn't even blink. "It's okay, Candi. I don't mind talking about it. At first it was hard, but I've worked through it." She paused for a moment to organize her thoughts, then continued: "Now, to answer your question. Jamie is autistic. Do you know what autism is?"

"I think so. It's a communication disorder, isn't it? I've read something about it. And I seem to recall a couple of court cases that involved autistic children. The main thing I remember is that autistic people don't talk and they don't interact much with other people."

"That's autism, all right. And that's what Jamie has." Marianne pulled up in front of Candi's condominium and turned into the driveway. She put the van in park, and, when her companion made no move to get out of the car, she shut off the engine. Candi turned to look at Jamie in the back seat. He was sitting quietly, staring out the window into her front yard. He wasn't fussing any more; apparently the unexpected change in route had been forgotten. Candi watched him intently for a few moments. Then she turned back to Marianne.

"How are you handling this problem, Marianne?" she asked. "It must be kind of an adjustment to find out that one of your children is autistic." Candi was a professional woman, and she was accustomed to getting right to the point. However, Marianne was not intimidated by the question.

"It was an adjustment, all right. Pretty tough at first." Marianne sighed and looked back over her shoulder at her son. "But now it's easier. I've changed my priorities quite a bit during the last six months. I quit my job—I just do an occasional house here and there—so I can spend more time with Jamie. I got him into a special pre-school program for children with disabilities. He goes there three times a week. I bought a tutoring kit so I could teach him words and numbers at home. It feels good just to be doing something. You know what I mean?"

Candi nodded. After a moment, she probed some more: "What's the long-term prognosis for Jamie? Will he ever be able to function normally?"

"I don't know. From what I've been able to find out, some autistic children—the high-functioning ones—do pretty well;

they can take care of themselves when they're older and live fairly independently. Others need lots of help all through their lives. And it's hard to predict where a specific child will be ten years or twenty years down the road. That's one of the things that makes it so challenging. We really don't know how Jamie will do. He's just four-and-a-half years old, so there's a lot of waiting ahead. I guess we just have to live one day at a time. I don't know how much I can do to help him, but I'm sure going to try. Jamie deserves a chance. Who knows, maybe he'll surprise us." Marianne managed another smile.

Candi returned the smile. She reached over and put her hand on Marianne's arm. "Thanks for telling me about him. I suppose people must ask about this a lot. You probably dread talking about it."

"Actually, most people *don't* ask about Jamie. I don't know if they don't know or if they don't care or if they just don't know how to ask. Everyone has problems, you know. Except for Brian, I really don't talk to people very much about my son. It's been nice to talk to you, Candi."

"And I've enjoyed talking to you." Candi turned for a last look at Jamie. Reaching over the seat, she patted him on the shoulder. As he squirmed away, she said, "Bye, Jamie. You take good care of your mom, okay?" Giving Marianne another squeeze on the arm, she slid out the door. "Bye, Marianne. I feel like I've made a new friend today. Jamie and I will be good buddies."

"I'm glad. Jamie may not be your average child, but, in his own way, he's a special little guy."

"I know."

♦♦♦

Marianne pulled into the driveway of her home in Woodbrook Court. Contrasts of earth, brick, and sky caught her eye on what had turned out to be a beautiful spring morning, and she paused for a moment to admire the place where she had spent much of the last eight years of her life. A split-level with a brick facade in front and blue siding on the other three sides, the house lay at the foot of a gently sloping hill on the east side of Colorado Springs. A curved sidewalk turned left from the middle of the driveway to the front steps of the house. Two quaking aspen, their tiny leaves shimmering in the wind, dominated the garden area between the sidewalk and the front window. Recently planted petunias and marigolds peeked out of the dark soil around the trees, and an assortment of shrubs and bushes filled the perimeter along the edge of the house. The lawn, which sloped down to the street and around the edge of the house into the backyard, was already lush and green. Behind the house a covered patio cut into the side of the hill, edged by a wooden fence and the weed-covered slopes of the mountain.

When they bought the home in Woodbrook Court, the house was new but the yard was a wasteland of rocks and weeds. Marianne noted with satisfaction the result of years of careful cultivation. It wasn't fancy, but it was definitely attractive. To her, this place was more than a house. It was a piece of her life.

As soon as the garage door closed behind them, Marianne popped Jamie from his car seat and hustled him into the house. He was too big to carry, so she took him by the hand and pulled him behind her. When they reached the door, he squirmed out of her grasp and ran into the kitchen. He seemed happy to be home again.

"Let's get some lunch, Jamie," his mother said.

"Lunch," he repeated. Marianne made mental note of the word as she searched through the refrigerator for leftovers. She made a note of *every* word these days.

Moments later the two of them sat down to ham and cheese sandwiches, green beans warmed up from a can, and what remained of a casserole from the night before. Marianne poured Jamie a glass of milk. "Well, Jamie," she said, "Do you like your lunch?"

The boy looked up when he heard his name, glanced briefly at his mother, and took another big bite out of his sandwich.

Everything was disappearing rapidly from his plate—the casserole, the sandwich, the green beans . . .

My gosh, this kid eats vegetables! Marianne realized with a start. She knew that Jamie was a good eater, but the universality of his appetite had never impressed her like this before. She found herself comparing him to her other children. Jamie obviously hadn't learned that the only things that tasted good were ice cream and pizza. She smiled at the thought.

Jamie ate everything on his plate long before Marianne had finished hers. He turned to his mother. "Mo," he said in a loud voice. The intonation was altogether unnatural, but Marianne knew exactly what he meant, and rewarded him with another helping of the casserole. Like a back-hoe digging a trench for a water main, he thrust his spoon into the casserole and stuffed it into his mouth. He finished that portion in twenty-three seconds. Marianne knew it was exactly twenty-three seconds because she was tracking it on the clock.

Jamie may be autistic but he's certainly not anorexic, she concluded as the boy hopped off his stool and trotted over to the cookie jar for his favorite treat. She found comfort in knowing that physically he was pretty much like any other four-year-old child.

Marianne got up from her chair and began clearing the table. It took only a few minutes to put the dishes in the sink and wipe off the table. That was the beauty of leftovers. It also helped to have only two people eating lunch. She realized, with just a touch of regret, that she was spending a lot of her time these days fixing and cleaning up meals. A vision of the real estate office passed through her mind, then faded away—just one of many things that had changed in her life in recent months. She reminded herself that she was doing what she needed to do. She was doing what she *wanted* to do.

Marianne opened the front door and walked outside to check the mailbox. She found three letters. The first letter was the monthly phone bill. She tossed it on the table. The second was a fat envelope with an offer for a new credit card. She tore it up and threw it into the waste basket. The third letter looked more interesting. At least it had a personalized return address. She looked at the name. Frances Jacobson. The name meant nothing to her but it did stir up a little curiosity. She opened the envelope by tearing off the right edge, then removed the letter and unfolded it. After peeking into Jamie's room to make sure he was all right, she sat down at the kitchen table to read the letter.

An invitation to Cherry Creek High School Class of '64 twenty year reunion — that's what it was. And Frances Jacobson turned out to be Frances *Smith* Jacobson. Of course. The senior class president. She was writing in behalf of the twenty-year reunion committee.

Had it really been twenty years? Marianne shook her head as she searched the letter for details. Two days of activities were planned for the first weekend in August, including a tour of the high school and the recently added south wing. The big event was a dinner-dance at a posh restaurant in Denver. A family picnic at the park was also on the agenda.

Family picnic? She thought about that one for a moment. How would such an activity turn out for a family like . . . like her family? If they went, would they take Jamie? How would he act in that crowd of unfamiliar people? And what if there was a dog at the park and he ran screaming back to the car?

It wouldn't be any different for me than for any other mother with a small child, she told herself, but she only half believed it. Marianne had had considerable experience already trying to deal with Jamie's unorthodox behavior at social events; she didn't want to go through that again if she and Brian went to the reunion. She finally decided it would be easier not to go. Her current personal friends didn't include anyone from her high school class, anyway.

Marianne went into the living room and sat down on the couch. High school days were on her mind; she found herself sifting through old memories. She tried to remember what classes she had taken in twelfth grade. The junior prom passed before her mind's eye in a flashback garnished with crepe and swirling music. She thought in turn of Larry, Pam, Jackie — friends who now lived only in scattered memories.

She thought of the plays and performances. Drama and music were her thing in high school. She had played Elaine in *Arsenic and Old Lace*; Penny in *June Mad*; Miss Sheffield in the senior class assembly. And what of her friends in the orchestra, the practices and performances, the solo night when she had played Faure's *Elegy*? Those were good times. Somehow, they seemed so long ago right now.

Marianne's reverie dissolved when she discovered a little body standing in the entrance to the living room. She watched Jamie as he advanced slowly toward her. He was carrying a wire clothes hanger that he had picked up somewhere. She noticed the clothes hanger right away because he was flipping it vigorously, snapping it repeatedly against his wrist.

He'll never be in a play, she thought darkly. Then, softening to the need she sensed in the child, she held out her arms and called gently, "Jamie. Jamie. Come to me, sweetheart."

Jamie stopped just outside the reach of her outstretched arms. He stood there watching her. The clothes hanger ceased its frantic vibration for a few seconds. Then he backed away and started flipping it again.

Marianne sensed conflict. She felt that Jamie was being tugged toward her and away from her, fear and desire in opposition. She wanted very much to tip the balance in her favor. *Don't make any sudden moves,* a voice whispered inside her head. So she waited patiently. Jamie was still standing in the same spot, alternatively flipping the hanger and then holding it still.

Marianne began speaking again, softly and deliberately. "Jamie," she said. "Do you know who I am? I'm your mommy. You're my little boy. I love you, Jamie. I want to help you. Please let me help you, Jamie."

Marianne pointed to herself. "Mommy," she said in a straight, even tone. Jamie looked at her, not into her eyes, but at her face. He was completely still now.

She pointed again. "Mommy."

The boy's lips trembled. He seemed to be concentrating, trying to form a word. Marianne said the word once more: "Mommy." She waited breathlessly for what seemed like an eternity.

"Mah . . . mi." He voiced the word imperfectly, with an unnatural break between the syllables. But there was no mistaking the word or the meaning. To Marianne the short utterance was like a small cloud that momentarily shields the burning sun on a hot summer afternoon.

In an instant, Jamie turned and was gone.

His mother was crying.

✦✦✦

Eager to take advantage of what time remained before her children and husband came home from school, Marianne changed into sweats and sneakers and climbed onto the exercise bicycle in the family room. She set the timer for twenty minutes and began pumping. As she pedaled, her mind drifted back to her conversation with Candi. She began to wonder if she had handled that situation right. Did she say too much? She wondered if she had come across as overly dramatic, too anxious to talk about the challenges of having a handicapped child. After all, other people had their problems, too. Maybe she was making too much out of it. Then again, it was kind of a big deal. Frightening for the present, terrifying for the future. Like she had told Candi, there was no way of knowing what would happen in ten or twenty years. She decided that uncertainty was the worst thing of all.

If only there were something she could hope for.

She was perspiring now. She pedaled faster, pushing her legs into the bicycle. It felt good to push.

There was that word that Jamie had spoken in the living room. Granted, she had heard him say other words in the past.

But usually they were just echoes or ritualistic expressions. This one had been different. Jamie hadn't just said "mommy." He had called *her* mommy. If he could do that, couldn't he learn other things as well? Maybe it would take him a little longer, but he could do it, especially with extra help. *She* would provide that help. She put her feet firmly into the pedals again and fought her way forward.

As soon as she finished exercising, Marianne headed up the stairs to find Jamie. He was not in his room so she began checking out the rest of the house. She found him, not inside the house, but in the backyard in his sandbox. The little boy had a spoon in his left hand. He was scooping up the sand and tossing big clumps of it into the air. Some of it had settled in his hair and on his clothes. But his mother resisted the temptation to clean him off. Instead, she stopped at the edge of the sand pile, crouched down to put herself at his level, and studied him intently in order to reassess his potential.

Jamie paid no attention to her. He continued clawing at the dirt. He had now created a little hole in the sand. He was looking at the hole, apparently intrigued by the results of his efforts.

Marianne continued to watch. She looked at the curly brown hair on the top of Jamie's head. Right now it looked more like a dirty mop rag. She searched his face, finding little expression or emotion there. She gazed intently at his eyes, as if to measure the intelligence within by looking through those two small windows. He averted her gaze, and in the end there was little to be learned from the eyes. Jamie's mind remained a mystery to his mother. She wished she could reach her hands inside the little head and rearrange whatever was in disarray there.

Instead, she reached out in the only way she could — with her arms. She put her hands around Jamie's waist and lifted him up. Then she pressed him close against her breast, curving her arms around his body and squeezing him tightly, pressing his cheek against her own. "Jamie," she said. "I love you."

There was a piercing scream. Like an insect trapped in a bottle, the little body writhed and squirmed and pushed away from his mother's embrace. Startled, Marianne dropped him to the ground. Thrusting her hands away, he retreated back into the sandbox. He stood there for a moment, panting heavily and crying softly. Then he sat down in the sand and began digging again.

Marianne turned away and walked slowly back to the house. For the second time that afternoon, she was crying.

Chapter Five
May 1984

Jamie's little head swayed back and forth, rhythmically following the cars as they whizzed by in a parade of colors and sounds. He followed each car until it disappeared down the road. Then he turned his eyes eagerly ahead to find the next one.

Car.

There was a yellow line in the middle of the road. Sometimes the line stayed in the same place. Sometimes it moved underneath the car or away from it. Watching the yellow line made him feel good because it was familiar, because he knew he was going home. Jamie liked going home. He squealed and pulled himself up in his car seat.

Suddenly, everything changed. The comfortable, familiar street was gone. Jamie knew it instantly. A strange new scene flooded his senses and a knot formed in his stomach. He screamed, then whimpered quietly as the frightening sensations gradually subsided.

Jamie wanted to go home. He knew he was going somewhere else, and he didn't like it. He wanted his road back.

The car stopped and he looked out the window. He saw a house. Jamie knew it wasn't his house and he knew they weren't going to stay there. He felt better now. He knew they would soon go back to the familiar road that would take him home.

A dog came around the side of the house, stopped on the front lawn and looked at the van. Jamie saw the dog right away and pulled back instinctively. He disliked dogs very much. Dogs and cats. He was afraid of them, though he was not too afraid right now because there was a window between him and the dog. Fascinated and fearful, he watched the dog carefully for a while.

When the car started moving once more, Jamie stared at the road again. Soon it changed back into the familiar road. He relaxed. Now he felt warm and comfortable again because he was going home.

Home.

Jamie smiled when the blue van pulled up in front of his house and turned into the driveway. He was already fumbling with the buckle on his car seat when the person in the front seat reached back to help him unbuckle it. He allowed the person to take his hand and help him out of the car, but as soon as he could he pulled free and ran into the kitchen. He knew the way.

Jamie was still thinking about the ride in the car. In his mind he could see the black road with the yellow line. He saw the cars going by. Thinking about the road and the cars made him feel good. He didn't remember the little side trip.

Now the person was speaking to him. Among many unfamiliar words was one that caught his attention. When he heard "Lunch," Jamie forgot about the road and the cars. He repeated the word: "Lunch." He began to think about some of his favorite kinds of food: sandwiches, soup, carrot sticks, cookies. He didn't think about cereal or scrambled eggs, because those things were for breakfast. He knew the difference between lunch and breakfast.

Lunch.

Jamie climbed up on his stool and sat down. He watched the food being prepared. He was hungry. The person put a sandwich on his plate, then some casserole and green beans. He stuffed the food into his mouth and swallowed it quickly.

When it was gone, he wanted more. He tried to get the person's attention. "Mo," he said. When he got more food, he ate that, too. Then he hopped down from his stool and went to get a cookie. Jamie liked cookies. Going to the cookie jar was one of his favorite things. He did it every day at lunch. It made him feel good to know that the cookie jar would always be there.

After lunch Jamie went into his room. Kneeling down and reaching under the bed, he pulled out the board with the big loader on it. The big loader went around a track and moved tiny plastic balls from one place to another. He always played with it after lunch. He put the big loader on the track and turned on the switch. He watched it go around. When it dropped the plastic balls into the bin above the track, he giggled.

Big loader.

Suddenly the big loader stopped. Jamie pushed it, but nothing happened. He picked it up and flipped the switch back and forth. It still wouldn't go. Finally he hurled the big loader to the floor and grunted in dismay. Then he stood up and began pacing around the room.

A clothes hanger that had been left on his bed caught his attention. He didn't know what it was, but he picked it up and looked it over. He began flipping it back and forth in his hand. The clothes hanger felt good each time he felt it move in his hand. He needed the hanger because he was upset about the big loader not working.

After a few minutes Jamie left his room and went into the kitchen. From there he wandered into the living room, but he stopped when he saw the person on the couch. He preferred being alone. He stayed in the entrance to the living room, flipping the clothes hanger in his hand. He couldn't decide whether to go into the living room.

The person said a word: "Jamie." He knew that word. He stopped flipping the hanger and looked at the person. He didn't look right at it because the eyes frightened him; he looked at the side of its face. Slowly he walked toward the person, stopping before he got too close. The person's arms were pointing at him. He twitched and began flipping the hanger vigorously. But he didn't run away.

"Jamie . . . " The person was still talking to him and looking at him. He liked that word. Somehow he knew it was his word. As he listened to the word again, it soothed him and made him feel better.

Jamie.

The person pointed a finger at its face. He heard it say something: "Mommy." This was a different word. He looked at the person as it said the word again: "Mommy." Jamie liked this word, too. It seemed familiar, but he didn't know what it meant. He wanted to know. As he looked at the person and listened to the sound of its voice, something clicked in his mind. All at once he knew.

The word was the person.

Jamie liked the word and he wanted to say it. He moved his lips, but his mouth was clumsy and mushy. "Mm," he mumbled. When the person repeated the word again, he tried once more to say it. "Mahmi," he said as he looked at the person.

Mommy.

The warm feeling was powerful now. He wanted to go closer. For just a moment, he wanted his mommy more than he wanted the big loader, more than he wanted the cars, even more than he wanted his lunch. He wanted *her.* But he couldn't move. He stood there, trying to look and not look, to feel and not feel, to move and not move. Then the warm feeling began to fade. He stepped back, and the switch that had turned on in his mind clicked back into its usual position.

He turned around and walked out of the room.

✦✦✦

Time slowed as the tiny pieces of sand floated through the air, frozen seconds in the hourglass of eternity. Jamie watched them drift effortlessly through the air in a white cloud. Watching them fall made him feel warm and tingly. Sand was nice; it was something he could depend on.

Sand.

When the air cleared, he scooped up another spoonful of the white grains and flung it gleefully into the air above his head. Once again the falling sand soothed him, though a few particles lodged in his eyes, causing some temporary discomfort. The top of his head was quite brown and dirty, but he didn't worry about that. He poked his spoon under another mound of sand and was just ready to toss it into the air when he saw the person. It was standing by his sandbox.

The person was looking at him. He saw the eyes, and they made him uncomfortable. He looked at the sand, focusing on the point where his little spoon broke the surface of the ground, waiting to see what the eyes would do.

"Jamie," a voice said. He heard some more words. The words were far away, disconnected from him. Then he felt himself grasped around the waist and lifted up. Strong hands crushed him. Something touched his cheek and a thousand needles pricked his face. He recoiled in horror. His skin was alive; wherever the person touched him, it burned like fire. A heavy shroud closed around him, squeezing his chest so he couldn't breathe. Jamie began thrashing wildly, kicking with his legs and pounding with his fists. He was suffocating, choking, burning. He had to get free.

Then the arms released him and the skin that was like a branding iron pulled away from his cheek. He was standing by himself in the sandbox. The prickly pain and suffocating sensation were subsiding.

Jamie quivered one last time. Still whimpering softly, he squatted down in the sand and pulled his spoon out of the dirt. He reached out to take a spoonful of sand. He could already feel the white crystals cascading around his head. The gentle, soothing sand . . .

Chapter Six
October 1986

Like Christmas, sixth period delayed its coming until the last possible moment. When it finally arrived, Brian faced it with more resignation than enthusiasm. Tired and suffering with a headache, he was glad that the last hurdle of the afternoon was in sight.

Room 19 had a worn look about it as well. The paint on the walls looked faded, some of the linoleum tiles on the floor were smooth and shiny, and one of the ceiling lights had burned out. The empty desks, their curved arms waiting to embrace the students when they arrived, stood silent and still as a herd of cattle sleeping on their feet. The whole room seemed to have aged during the day. It was enough to make anyone feel tired.

The sound of shuffling feet in the doorway announced the arrival of the students. Brian watched them file into the classroom and sprawl into their desks. They looked tired, too. He tried to think of something he could do to liven things up. Perhaps a little drama would help.

Sixth period was a twelfth grade English class. Today they were scheduled to finish *Macbeth* and take an exam on it. As soon as the bell rang and everyone was seated, Brian opened his world literature text to the last scene of the Shakespearean play and instructed the students to turn to the same page. "We're going to read the ending of the play together," he explained. "Who would like to read one of the parts?

This could be your big chance to launch your acting career." Several hands went up. Brian selected three boys and two girls to read the parts of Macbeth, MacDuff, Malcolm, Siward, and Ross, respectively.

The students read slowly, sometimes awkwardly, as they stumbled over the unfamiliar words, but with an occasional prompt they made it all the way through the final scene. By the time they finished reading, many of the other students appeared bored or restless, whispering softly to each other about topics that had little to do with *Macbeth*. Brian was not surprised. He was an experienced teacher; he knew what to expect from high school students, and he knew exactly what to do next.

"How many of you have seen this play performed on the stage?" he asked in a voice loud enough to command attention but soft enough to suggest that everything was under control. Two hands went up. "What did you think of it, Karen?" he asked a dark-haired girl on the front row.

"It was okay," she answered.

He followed up. "What did you learn from seeing *Macbeth*, Karen? What's the point of this play?"

The dark-haired girl thought for a moment. "Well, isn't it about how wanting power and money can ruin your life?" She looked at her teacher for confirmation.

"Excellent," he replied. He shifted his attention back to the entire class. "Let's review what happens in the play," he suggested. "Macbeth, a trusted friend of the king, becomes ambitious. Encouraged by Lady Macbeth, he resorts to treason and murder to get power. In the process he destroys himself and other people as well. Makes for a great plot. Unfortunately, there are plenty of historical accounts to show that this lust for power isn't limited to plays. For example, that's basically what happened in Nazi Germany to start the Second World War, isn't it? You see, Shakespeare isn't just entertaining us; he's telling us something important about human nature. Good point, Karen."

Brian paused and looked around the room. "Now let's explore this a little further," he said. "What else can we learn from *Macbeth?*"

"Stay away from witches," a deep, guttural voice called out from the back of the room. Andy Phillips' voice. Almost everyone laughed, including Brian. He waited a few moments for the students to quiet down, then continued: "Anything else?"

Jennifer Hansen raised her hand. Jennifer was one of the better scholars in the class of '87, the kind of student who makes teachers' lives a little easier. After receiving permission to speak, she said: "Mr. Spencer, I've been reading *Macbeth* for a couple of weeks now. You want to know what I think of it? I think it's depressing."

Brian smiled. "Please explain what you mean, Jennifer," he said.

"Well, it just seems like this play is mostly about bad things happening to people. You know, people getting killed, witches casting spells, everybody betraying each other. That sort of thing. A lot of movies are like that, too, but you don't take them as seriously. Reading *Macbeth* leaves you feeling kind of discouraged about life in general. You know what I mean?"

"I think so," Brian answered. He wasn't feeling quite so tired now and had forgotten about his headache. This discussion was taking an interesting turn, and he liked the possibilities. "You're saying that the tone of the play is kind of pessimistic," he restated.

"Yeah. And now this is the thing. I was wondering why Shakespeare is always so negative. Why did he write so many tragedies, anyway?"

"Well, that's a good question. And you're right, Shakespeare did write a lot of tragedies. If any of you ever have a chance to see *King Lear*, you'll find that it's even more depressing than *Macbeth*. But" — Brian paused for emphasis — "he wrote a lot of comedies, too."

He paused again and scanned the classroom to see what the other students were doing. A few were talking among themselves; others looked a little spacey—perhaps they were already hearing the end-of-class bell in their minds—but most appeared to be listening to the discussion. "Okay, class," he said. "How about it? Why did William Shakespeare write so many tragedies? Does he believe that life is inherently bad? Is he just trying to be sensational? What do you think?"

This time several students raised their hands. Brian called on Rob Baker. "Well, life can be pretty tough," Rob commented thoughtfully. "Bad things happen all the time. Maybe Shakespeare is just trying to be realistic."

"I'm sure that's part of it," Brian agreed. "Life's full of problems, isn't it? Bad things happen to good people. In other words, we all experience adversity. Let me read what Shakespeare said about adversity." Brian found his copy of *Shakespeare: The Complete Works*, leafed through it until he found the page he was looking for, and read:

> Sweet are the uses of adversity,
> Which, like the toad, ugly and venomous,
> Wears yet a precious jewel in his head.

He paused briefly, read the quote again, then said: "That's from *As You Like It*. Has anyone heard these lines before? What do they mean?" He paused again and waited for a response.

It was Jennifer Hansen who finally answered. "I don't think I understand the part about the toad," she said, "but is he saying that adversity, even though it seems bad, can sometimes cause good things to happen?"

"That's right, Jennifer," he said, nodding emphatically. "Let me tell you about the toad. You see, toads have a little gland in their heads that produces a foul-smelling, poisonous substance. It helps deter other animals from eating them. Now, in Shakespeare's time there was a widespread belief that this repulsive organ in the toad's head could cure all kinds of diseases. That's why they called it a 'jewel.' Adversity is like that: something good grows out of something distasteful. Think about it. The discouragement of defeat helps us enjoy the elation of victory; feeling sick and miserable at times makes us appreciate good health; anger and rejection teach us what love is. All this opposition we experience makes us stronger, and there is no greater satisfaction in life than knowing that we have faced a tough challenge and overcome it."

Brian walked back to his desk and replaced the book he had been reading from. "Good discussion, class," he concluded. He glanced at the clock. "And it looks like it's about time for the test." He stood up and walked around to the other corner of his desk where the exams were neatly stacked.

He passed out the exam. It was mostly multiple choice, with an essay question at the end. While the students worked through the items, Brian sat down at his desk and kept an eye out for hands of students with questions.

When the bell rang, the students got up immediately and filed noisily out of the room, leaving their completed exams face down on their desks. Three or four students were still writing the essay question as Brian walked up and down the rows, retrieving the tests and stacking them again on the corner of his desk.

When he turned around to check on the progress of the remaining students, Tracy Bradford was waiting to talk to him. "Mr. Spencer," Tracy began, "I have a couple of questions about the research paper. You know, the one that's due before Thanksgiving."

Brian sat down on the side of his desk and motioned for Tracy to come closer. "Well," he replied. "I must say I'm pleased to have someone working on the research paper already. I suspect most of the class don't even realize there *is* a research paper due in November. I was going to talk about it in class next week, but I'll be glad to answer any questions you have right now, so you can get started right away if you want."

Tracy opened his loose leaf binder, searching for the course outline. He was a conscientious student, and Brian could easily imagine his spending days or weeks on an assignment. Finally he found the paper he was looking for.

"Here it just says that we do this paper and it should be 10-12 pages long. What I was wondering is what we're supposed to write about. It doesn't say if it is about something we're studying in class, or what."

"As a matter of fact, you can write about any subject you're interested in, Tracy. The purpose of the assignment is to give you experience doing the research and writing the paper. You could write about something you've studied in science, for example; or maybe do research on a famous person who lived in the past; or whatever else interests you. Like I said, the purpose is just to learn how to write a research paper."

"Yeah. Well, I guess that's the other thing I don't understand. I don't think I've ever written anything this big before. I was kind of wondering how to do it. It sounds like it might take some time, so I wanted to get started on it."

"It's an excellent idea to get started right away. This kind of project isn't hard to do if you work away at it over several weeks. If you wait until the night before it's due and stay up all night writing the paper — which is the way a lot of students do it — well, that's the hard way." Brian smiled at Tracy. "When I talk to the class about this assignment next week, I plan to take some time to go through each step and explain how to do it. We'll talk about where to go for information, how to put notes on cards so you can remember them, how to organize the paper, and how to write it. In the meantime, why don't you be thinking of what you want to write about — maybe even start looking for books or articles that you could use in the paper. You should have plenty of time to put it together if you just follow the schedule I give you next week. I think you'll be in good shape, Tracy. You always do good work."

Tracy beamed at the compliment. "Okay," he said. "I'll do some thinking about my research paper, but I'll wait till after next week to start working on it." Tracy closed his loose leaf and turned to leave. He looked relieved. As he walked to the door, he turned to look over his shoulder. "Thanks, Mr. Spencer," he said.

◆◆◆

When Tracy had gone and the classroom was quiet, Brian remained for a time at his desk. Leaning back in his chair and resting his head against the wall, he tried to let his body and mind relax. He thought about all the Tracys and Jennifers he had taught over the years. Some of them were out of college now and well into their own careers. He had an investment in them. They were where they were partly because they learned how to write a research paper in Mr. Spencer's English class. Perhaps this low-profile, thankless profession of his was worth something after all.

After a while Brian got up and began putting the room in order so he could leave. But then, on his desk he found a paper from the principal's office—a request to nominate a student of the week from one of his classes. He picked up the form, wrote a name in the box, and went to the principal's office to deliver it. The building was mostly deserted by now; a few students congregated at their lockers or huddled around tables in the lunch room. Brian waved to some of them as he passed. He walked into the principal's office, dropped the request form on the secretary's desk, and stepped back into the hallway. That's where he ran into Carl Jackson.

Mr. Jackson was just emerging from the teacher's lounge when Brian came by. Fifteen years Brian's senior, Carl was one of the old guard at Palmer High School. It seemed he had been teaching math and biology to high school students since the invention of calculus. He was regarded as something of a sage.

He was also a big-time fan of the Denver Broncos.

"Well, Spencer," he chirped as Brian approached. "What did you think of the game last night?"

Brian knew what "the game" was, though he had not seen it personally. On that particular Monday night, while the Broncos fought the Forty-Niners, he had elected to wrestle with a stack of student essays. It would be easy to spend way too much time watching football so he tried to limit himself to the Saturday college games — at least until the playoffs. In any case, he thought wryly, he had fared better in his previous night's battle than the guys in the orange jerseys. However, he wasn't about to say that and risk a head-on confrontation. So he kept it simple.

"We lost."

"You might say that." Carl matched Brian's stride for a few seconds. Then he stopped walking and moved to one side of the hallway. Shifting his weight to his left foot, he braced himself against the wall. With his right toe, he traced the design in the tiles on the floor. He had planted himself. He wanted to talk.

Brian halted, too, and waited politely for the other man to speak. He anticipated receiving a blow-by-blow account and critique of the game. Instead, the conversation took on a decidedly businesslike tone.

"Brian, I've been looking for a chance to talk to you. Uh, you probably know we have a little committee organized to promote support for the school bond issue that's on the election ballot next month. I was wondering if you would be willing to help."

"What would you like me to do?"

"Well, the PTA has printed up a brochure that outlines the needs of the schools. We plan to canvas the area covered by Palmer High next week and get these booklets out to the homes. We have a lot of students to help us, so I don't think it will be too bad. But we could use your help for a couple of hours supervising some of the students who deliver the brochures."

"I think I could probably handle that."

"Thanks. I'll get back to you next week with the details." Carl had finished his request, but his body position suggested that he wasn't through talking. He didn't say anything else right away. He held his post by the wall, continuing to trace designs on the floor with his toe. Brian had just about decided to say good-bye and slip away when the other man asked another question.

"Do you remember my son, Corey?"

Brian didn't know a lot about Carl Jackson's family. He tried to remember. Two children: a girl and a boy. The girl was older and married. The boy was probably a senior in high school or maybe just graduated. But he didn't know either of them personally.

Carl picked up on the other's hesitation. "Don't remember him, huh? I thought he had you for English last year, but maybe it was someone else."

"Must have been. To be honest, I haven't had Corey in any of my classes and I'm not sure I'd even recognize him if I saw him. But I know who he is. One of the top students in the school, as I recall."

"Yeah. Well, I thought somehow you knew him."

"You were going to tell me something about him?"

"I was just going to tell you that he got a scholarship to Stanford. I was thinking you might be interested to know that because I thought you had been one of his teachers. Anyway, the kid has done well. We're proud of him."

"You should be. That's a great achievement. I hope things turn out well for him." That seemed to be a decent place to end the conversation, so Brian excused himself and walked back to his classroom. He sat down at his desk and leaned back in the chair.

Stanford. That was pretty incredible. Anyone could be proud of a son like that. He thought of his own son and winced at the comparison; James Spencer would never go to Stanford.

He caught himself. He had decided long ago that he would not overreact to Jamie's situation. It didn't work to compare him with other kids because he wasn't like other kids. He had to judge Jamie's life by a different set of criteria. He reminded himself that he didn't want to feel resentful or jealous. Jamie might never go to college, but there was a purpose for his life.

Something good would come from *this* adversity. He had to believe that.

After a few minutes he stood up and moved away from his desk. He checked the classroom to make sure everything was in order. Then, picking up the exams to correct at home, he went back into the long hallway and walked slowly to the end. He leaned hard on the horizontal bar that opened the front door of the high school and stepped out onto the sidewalk. A light breeze swept across the lawn, cool with the promise of winter. A large maple tree, its leaves aflame with autumn colors, rustled softly in the wind. Brian buttoned his sweater. He paused for a moment to savor the soothing movement of the maple leaves. Then he turned away and started home.

Chapter Seven
March 1989

Click.

Brian awoke slowly, puzzled by the strange sound hanging at the edge of his consciousness. It was not loud enough to have roused him, but now that he was awake he heard it distinctly — a squeaky noise that came at recurring, though not totally predictable, intervals.

Click.

He glanced at the LED on the clock. 2:53 a.m. The middle of the night. He lay in bed for awhile waiting to see if the strange sound would stop, but it persisted. There was nothing ominous about it, but at last curiosity got him to his feet and out into the hallway to investigate.

Light shone through the partially open doorway to Jamie's bedroom. That seemed unusual for this time of night. He moved slowly toward the room. He heard the clicking sound again and in the same instant the light disappeared.

So that was it. Someone was turning the light on and off in Jamie's room. The strange noise was caused by a squeaky light switch.

Brian crept up to the doorway and peeked inside the room. His eyes found Jamie's boyish body in the darkness. He was standing by the window, hunched over, rubbing his thighs with his hands and peering out the window through the vinyl blinds. After a couple of minutes Jamie turned and walked across the room. He stopped next to the door, reached up and flicked on the light. Then he retraced his steps to the window and looked out into the night.

Brian stayed at the door for several minutes. Fascinated, he watched Jamie do a strange ritual over and over: turn the light on; go to the window; look out the window; return to the light switch; turn off the light; return to the window. In his nine years with Jamie, Brian had never seen anything quite like this. Another surprise. The first thing that came to his mind was a question.

Why?

He knew he couldn't answer that question. Instead, he pushed the door open wider and stepped into the room.

"Jamie. It's not morning yet, son. You need to go back to bed."

Jamie glanced at his father and shuffled back over to the window. Brian moved to intercept him. Taking the boy by the hand and guiding him gently toward the bed, Brian whispered, "Come on Jamie. Let's put you back in bed. It's not time to get up yet."

"Nokay." Jamie stiffened and leaned back toward the window.

Brian took Jamie's hand again and pulled him toward the bed. He could feel resistance in the boy's body. Then, suddenly, the little body relaxed. Brian helped him get into bed. He backed away and watched for a few minutes to see if Jamie would stay in bed. Then he turned off the light—hopefully for the last time that night—and returned to his own bedroom.

As he hurried across the bedroom to get back into bed, Brian slammed his right foot into the leg of the chair that was pushed up under the desk. He grabbed the offended toe and cried out in pain. Then he lost his balance and toppled over, crashing into the desk. Something soft and sticky crunched under his hand as another object flew from the desk and ricocheted off the wall. Brian steadied himself and took a few deep breaths as he waited for the pain to subside. Then he turned on the desk lamp to survey the damage.

The soft object crushed by his hand was a doughnut that had been left on a napkin on the desk. It was pretty well smashed. Brian dropped the doughnut into the wastebasked and licked the frosting off his hand. He was more concerned about the other object. Dropping to his knees, he retrieved the gold pocket watch from the floor and held it up under the light. "You took quite a blow," he said as he inspected the delicate timepiece. Satisfied that nothing was damaged, he placed the watch carefully back on the desk. Then he turned off the light and tiptoed gingerly over to the bed, climbing in quietly so he wouldn't disturb Marianne. He lay there for a long time before he fell asleep, thinking about his still-throbbing toe and listening for clicking sounds.

✦✦✦

Brian slit open a new box of Cheerios and poured a generous helping into a bowl. He scooped up a handful and ate them plain. Then he added milk and sugar and was working his way through the rest of the bowl of cereal when Marianne came into the kitchen.

"Where's the checkbook?" she asked as she rustled through the papers and other odds and ends on the counter.

"Sorry. Haven't seen it," he replied. As she continued to search the drawers, the top of the refrigerator, and other nooks and crannies, he added, "Have you looked in your purse?"

"Yes, it's not there." She sighed. "Why do I always do this? I guess it'll probably show up somewhere." She gave up searching for the checkbook, went over to the table and sat down by her husband. "So how are you today, honey?" she asked, propping her head on her elbow and turning to look at him.

"Fine. A bit tired, but as soon as all this sugar kicks in I'll get going."

"Working too hard these days?" she asked matter-of-factly.

"I always work too hard," he teased. "But that's not what I meant. I was talking about loss-of-sleep tired."

Now she was curious. "What do you mean, 'loss-of-sleep tired'? You always sleep well. I should know after all these years of trying to wake you up on Saturday mornings. Did you get sick or something in the night?"

He pushed the empty cereal bowl away and began peeling a banana. The banana was quite ripe and several soft spots appeared as the skin dropped away. Taking a knife, Brian carved out the brown spots and bit off the end of the banana. Only then did he answer her question.

"I was up in the middle of the night with Jamie. He was turning the light off and on in his room. And he kept going over to the window and staring outside. It was weird. I don't know how long he would have stayed there if I hadn't come. I finally got him back in bed." Brian finished the banana. "Have you noticed anything like that before?"

"Yes." Marianne was looking away from him now and she was smiling.

"What have you seen?"

"Oh, just kind of like what you described. Jamie up in the night, walking around, doing things."

"Has this been going on long?"

"That particular behavior—the middle-of-the-night thing— has been going on for a couple of weeks." She got up from the table and walked over to the other side of the counter.

"It has? Why wasn't I aware of it? And what do you mean by 'that particular behavior'?"

"Brian, let's face it. You're not always in touch with what Jamie's doing." She began organizing the things on the top of the counter and clearing some of them away. "And that's to be expected. You're gone during the day, you have a lot of things to worry about, and you really do, uh, sleep well. I'm here with him all day and I have more opportunity to see what he does. The truth is, I've been kind of concerned about him. In the last few months it seems like he's been developing more and more of these rituals. What you saw last night is just one of the things he does. There's more. When he gets home from school he sits down over there by the sliding glass door and stares out into the backyard for awhile. I think maybe he watches the shadows when the sun is shining; but he does it when it's cloudy, too. He opens the dishwasher, piles the dishes on the counter, and then puts them back in the dishwasher. He gets out his toys in a certain order—first the train, then his cars, then the Legos. It's like he has to do these things as part of his day. And they have to be done in a certain order and at a certain time. If he gets disrupted he gets very upset. He's always had some of these ritualistic tendencies. You know that. But they seem to be getting worse lately."

Brian had finished eating. He was staring into the depths of what had once been his bowl of Cheerios, idly stirring a few remaining circles with his spoon. "So what do we do about these new things that Jamie's doing?" he asked. "Or do we need to do anything?"

"I don't know, Brian. I don't know what's going to happen. I do know that he's pretty hard to manage sometimes. I think we just have to take it a day at a time right now."

Brian looked at her and nodded. Rising from the table, he took his empty bowl to the dishwasher, gave Marianne a kiss on the cheek as he passed her, and went back to the bedroom to get dressed for work.

◆◆◆

By evening the middle-of-the-night episode with Jamie had been largely forgotten. Brian thought of it briefly when he went into the family room before dinner and saw Jamie there. He also remembered the commitment he had made to himself that very morning to get more involved. He went over to where Jamie was kneeling on the carpet in front of the television, busily rotating the channels and chuckling to himself whenever *Sesame Street* flashed by on the screen.

"Hi, Jamie," he said.

"Hi, Jamie," replied the boy without looking up from the TV.

"Hi, *dad,*" Brian corrected.

"Hi, dad," Jamie repeated in the same monotone voice.

"How was school today, Jamie? Did you have fun?"

"Fun," said Jamie. He began rocking back and forth on the floor, shaking his head vigorously. Brian interpreted this to mean that Jamie was not interested in talking to him right then. With a sigh, he patted his son on the head and left the room.

When he entered the kitchen he found Sara doing homework. He stopped for a moment and took a long look at the open textbook on the table.

"Looks like you're doing algebra," he observed.

"Algebra II," Sara corrected without looking up.

Brian whistled softly and raised his eyebrows. "Algebra II!" he repeated with pretended surprise. "In tenth grade? We didn't take Algebra II when I was in tenth grade."

"Dad, they didn't even have Algebra II when you were in tenth grade," Sara quipped, smiling at her own cleverness. "Plus a lot of other stuff. You're ancient, dad."

Brian laughed and threw up his hands. "Good comeback," he said as he walked away.

Later that evening he went back to the high school for a parent-teacher conference. Only a few parents showed up, but he met with each one of them individually and reviewed their students' progress. He got home late, skimmed the newspaper, and went to bed.

He awoke at 3:30; this time it was almost automatic, and he didn't like it. He tried to go right back to sleep, but found himself listening instead for unusual sounds in the night. Sure enough. There it was—the clicking noise. Like an unexpected reminder of an unpaid insurance premium, the squeaky sound purged the quiet forgetfulness of sleep from his mind and replaced it with unpleasant responsibilities. *Not again!* he thought. He lay there for a few minutes, listening to the now hateful sound, weighing the pros and cons of getting involved. Finally, he lifted himself reluctantly out of bed and headed for Jamie's room.

Jamie was parroting his routine of the previous night: turn on the light; walk to the window; look outside; return to the light switch; turn off the light; return to the window; look outside; return to the light switch. His movements were deliberate and measured, and possessed a kind of graceful, athletic quality, though there was something incongruous about them—like a boxer doing a ballet.

Jamie seemed entranced and stimulated by his little dance. Brian hesitated outside the door, reluctant to intervene. Then he remembered that this was his son, that he was still a boy, that he needed sleep, and that this strange behavior, left unchecked, would surely have negative consequences over time. So, for the second time in as many nights, he opened the door and faced his son.

"Hi, Jamie," he said, trying to appear calm and nonchalant. "It's not morning yet. Would you like to go back to bed now?"

Jamie paid no attention to him. He was looking out the window. The horizontal vinyl blinds were opened just enough for him to squint through. A moment later he abandoned his position by the window and glided toward the door and the light switch. Then the room went dark.

Brian decided to try again. "Jamie, you need to go back to bed. It's way too early to get up. You need to get some sleep." There was a little more authority in his voice now, a promise that additional methods would be employed if this new request were ignored.

It *was* ignored. Jamie turned from the light switch and went back to the window. Brian reached out and grabbed his hand, pulling him toward the bed. Jamie jerked away and squealed. He planted himself firmly in front of the window.

"I feel like the sorcerer's apprentice trying to stop the broom," Brian muttered to himself. He took hold of Jamie's arm, more firmly this time, and marched him over to the bed. Jamie screamed and tried to get away. Brian tried talking again. "Come on, Jamie. Please come to bed. It's not good for you to be doing this. You can't stay up all night. You've got to go back to bed. Come on, let's go."

No dice. Jamie fought him, twisting and jerking, trying to pry his father's fingers from his arm. Brian's anger flared. *This is so dumb,* he thought. What's wrong with this kid, anyway? "Jamie," he ordered. "Stop doing this!"

Jamie fought harder. He snorted and pranced around like an unbroken stallion, pushing and shoving in a frenzied effort to get away from his father. Brian put his arms behind Jamie's knees, lifted him up and dropped him firmly in the middle of the bed. Half a second later Jamie was back on his feet, racing toward the window. He stopped there—stoic and statuesque— and looked out into the blackness.

Brian was furious now. "Get back in bed!" he shouted. "I'm getting sick and tired of this." Jamie screamed and looked out the window. All at once Brian realized that his son was not going to move. Forcing himself to step back, he took a couple of deep breaths and tried to decide what to do.

"All right, Jamie," he said at last. "I guess you win. If you want to stay up all night and stand by that stupid window, I guess that's up to you." Pulling the door closed behind him, he strode out of the room and back to his own bedroom.

◆◆◆

When Brian awoke the next morning, he got out of bed and went directly to Jamie's room. He pushed the door open and peered inside. His heart despaired when he saw Jamie standing by the window. *He's been there all night,* he realized. He turned away with a new resolve to find a solution to this problem.

All day Brian was haunted by the image of a pathetic little figure endlessly pacing the floor or hovering by the window and staring glassy-eyed into the night. Every recollection of Jamie's troublesome behavior bothered him because he had no idea what to do about it. Equally disturbing were the questions it raised about his competence as a father. He was used to a Jamie who sat unobtrusively on the floor or wandered silently through the house with his carry-around toy. And if there had been little opportunity for interaction, at least there had been little conflict. Now, when he needed some father-to-son influence, his inability to relate to Jamie in any meaningful way was painfully obvious. He felt guilty for having drifted into a passive relationship with a son who was all too easily ignored.

Well, he wasn't ignoring him now. But whenever he thought about the previous night's experience and the futility of trying to negotiate with Jamie, he shook his head. Barring child abuse, there didn't seem to be any way to get Jamie to cooperate.

On his way home from work Brian had an idea. He would need Marianne's help to pull it off. After dinner, when Marianne was playing the piano, he crept up and sat down by her on the piano bench. Keeping a watchful eye on the moving hands, he put his arm around her shoulders, leaned over and kissed her on the ear. "Can I talk to you for a moment?" he whispered.

"Sure. Just give me a couple of minutes. Okay?" Maintaining her concentration, she finished the last sixteen measures of *Clair de Lune*, drawing a succession of sweet notes from the piano like candy from a valentine box. For a moment—mesmerized by the music and Marianne—Brian forgot what he had come for. Then Marianne turned away from the keyboard, gave him a triumphant smile, and said: "Your turn, now. What's up?"

Brian took a deep breath and tried to compose his thoughts. "Well," he said, "I guess you know that I've been up with Jamie the last couple of nights. Last night he was doing his window thing from at least 3:30 on. I tried to get him to go back to bed but he refused to do it. He was still there when I got up this morning. It just makes me sick to think of him pacing the floor and standing there by the window all night long. I think we need to do something about it."

"I'm concerned about Jamie's behavior, too," Marianne replied. "I've been up myself and seen him wandering around. But that's not the only peculiar thing he does."

"I know. But this is probably the most serious one, don't you think?"

She paused for a moment as if weighing his words. "Yes, I guess you're right," she said. "So what do you suggest?"

"Well, my idea is that if we can just disrupt this little ritual of his, we may be able to stop it. He seems to be caught up in the routine—you know, going through all the different steps. Everything is always done in the same order and he seems obsessed with going through the cycle over and over. If we can just break the cycle, maybe he'll be able to let go of it."

"Here's my plan. One of us needs to sleep in his room, probably on the floor by the window. If he gets up he won't be able to get to the window because we're there and then he'll give up and go back to bed. Easy as pie. However, we may need to do it several nights in a row, so maybe we should work together and take turns."

Marianne looked doubtful. "Well, I guess it's worth a try. Shall I be the first one to sleep there?"

Brian shrugged his shoulders. "It doesn't matter to me. I can go first. After all, it's my idea."

"No. I'd like to go first," she responded. "But only on one condition. I get to use one of the foam pads we bought for camping trips. My idea of sacrifice doesn't include hard floors."

He laughed. "It's a deal." Then he added, "I don't know if this will work, but it's good to be trying something, don't you think?"

Marianne nodded. She was trying to remember where she had put the foam pads.

✦✦✦

The cobwebs had barely melted from her mind when Marianne came awake with a start. Someone—or something—had stepped on her as she slept. At first she was frightened. Then she remembered where she was. In the dark she could just make out the form of a child standing at her feet.

"Jamie?"

She heard a squeal in response, and the shadowy form squeezed by her, moving gingerly across the bouncy foam pad to the window. Apparently, sleeping there didn't keep him away. She sat up in her makeshift bed, looked at her son, and began talking to him softly.

"Jamie, it's mommy. I want you to go back to bed, sweetheart. See, I'm sleeping here in your room, and I need you to go back to bed. Will you please go back to bed now?"

Jamie stuck his face closer to the window.

Marianne moved closer and put her arms around his waist. "Come on, Jamie. I'll help you back to bed." Jamie pulled away and walked over to the door. He turned the light on. He turned it off. Then he flicked it on again, turned around and looked at his mother. He obviously wanted to go back to the window, but he was displeased with the obstacle in his path.

Marianne was equally perplexed. What should she do now? She looked at Jamie. He began fidgeting. He started toward the window, then pulled back with a grunt and paced in circles by the door. He looked anything but tired and sleepy.

Marianne, on the other hand, was very tired. She could see a battle ahead and she had no relish for it. Uncertain how to proceed, she lay down on her portable bed, turned on her side so she could watch Jamie, and waited to see what would happen.

He snorted and pranced around a while longer. Then, apparently concluding that his mother was not going to move, he worked his way cautiously back toward the window. Stepping over the prostrate form, he put his face up against the blinds and looked out through the window.

Marianne got wearily to her feet. Taking Jamie by the hand, she led him over to the bed. He didn't fight or resist. She eased him down on the bed and stepped back.

He was back on his feet instantly, heading for the window. Marianne snagged him by the arm, and pulled him back to the bed again. This time she could feel more resistance.

Before he even reached a prone position, Jamie jumped up and escaped. Three seconds later he was back in front of the window, scattering the blankets on the foam pad.

Marianne turned and rushed out of the room. Moments later she was shaking her husband's sleeping form and pulling him out of bed. "All right, Houdini," she said. "This was your idea. I want to see what your trick is for getting it done!" Brian didn't bounce out of bed as enthusiastically as his son, but with Marianne's prodding he was soon standing by his wife at the door to Jamie's room.

"What happened?" he whispered as soon as his mind began to function.

"Nothing," she retorted. "That's the problem. Sleeping by the window did about as much good as waving a magic wand. I tried to get him back to bed, but it didn't work. Short of sitting on him all night, I have no idea how to stop him from getting up and running around."

Brian turned to look into the room. Jamie had resumed his routine, retracing the various steps with tireless precision. There was no indication that the confrontation with his mother had affected any aspect of the strange ritual.

"I still think we need to find some way to disrupt this routine," Brian said to himself. He turned back to his wife. "Marianne, I need you to help me. I'm going to pull Jamie out of his room into the hallway. Can you watch him here? I'm going to close the door and hold it from the inside so he can't get back in. Maybe if we keep him away from the light switch and the window we can disrupt what he's doing."

"Okay." She looked a little dubious, but added: "I'm willing to try anything at this point."

Opening the door, Brian stepped inside and walked over to his son. Jamie was standing by the window, eyes pressed close to the blinds, straining to see something in the darkness. Brian touched him gently on the shoulder. "Come on Jamie," he said quietly. "You have to go back to bed."

Jamie shrank back, arching his body to put space between himself and the annoying fingers. "Nokay," he said. He resumed his position by the window, trying to ignore his father.

Taking a deep breath, Brian took hold of Jamie's hands and pulled him slowly toward the open door. Surprisingly, the boy followed willingly. When they were out in the hallway he turned Jamie over to Marianne. She took him by both hands as Brian had done and waited to see what he would do.

"Jamie, you'll have to stay out here with mom until you're ready to go back to bed," Brian explained. "Are you ready to go back to bed now?"

Jamie began to squirm. He tried to pull away from his mother and go back into his room. When Marianne didn't let go, he became more agitated, pushing and pulling to get free.

"Jamie, you can't go back into your room unless you get into your bed." Brian's voice was firmer this time.

Jamie screamed and fought harder. He managed to free one of his hands. Then he cocked his arm and struck Marianne's arm with his fist. She winced and drew back instinctively.

Brian reacted immediately and forcefully. He grabbed Jamie by the shoulders and shook him. "Don't you hit your mother like that," he thundered. "Don't *ever* hit your mother like that!"

The harsh words and rough treatment struck Jamie like a jackhammer. The boy turned hysterical. He screamed and kicked, clawing with his hands and trying desperately to get away from his father.

"Brian," Marianne pleaded. "This isn't working. Please, if there's something else you planned to do, do it *now*. We can't stay here and fight him. It's useless."

Brian looked at Marianne. Thrusting Jamie back toward her, he darted quickly into Jamie's bedroom and closed the door. Then he sat down on the floor inside, back against the door and feet braced against the dresser.

On the other side of the door Jamie was out of control. He pushed against the door, trying to force it open. Then he beat on it with his fists and kicked it with his feet. Inside, Brian held his ground, wishing fervently that he could lock the door. Unfortunately, the doorknobs had been reversed a couple of years earlier so that Jamie could be locked *inside* his room during time-outs.

More than once the door gave way behind him as Jamie turned the door knob and pushed and shoved. The power in his small limbs was frightening to Marianne, who tried unsuccessfully to restrain him or to divert his attention away from the door. Like a caged animal trying to escape, the boy fought to get through the door. After a few minutes of useless pleading, Marianne finally withdrew and watched helplessly.

I could fight him, she said to herself, *but what good would that do? What can I to do? And why did Brian start this horrible thing, anyway?* She began to cry.

Jamie continued to scream and pound on the door. Each time the door slipped open a crack, Brian pushed it firmly back into place. He wondered why he was doing this; he also wondered if the door would break—but he did not relinquish his position. What began as a simple diversionary tactic had become a contest, a game to be won. It was father against son in an all-out battle to conquer the door, and there were no rules.

"Mom, what's going on out here?" Marianne looked up to see Angela's puffy eyes glaring at her. She looked bewildered and angry. It was not a happy face.

"I'm sorry, Angie," Marianne apologized. "We're trying to break Jamie of getting up and walking around in the middle of the night. I know it's kind of distracting."

"Distracting? It's disgusting. Mom, do you have to do this? Why don't you just leave Jamie alone and let him do his thing?"

Why not? Marianne wondered. Why were they putting themselves through this torture? It wasn't going to work, anyway. As soon as they left, he'd go right back to his *thing.*

"Please go back to bed, Angie. This won't last too long. I promise."

Angela turned and stormed back to her room. She slammed the door as she went through. Marianne sighed and turned back to Jamie. He was still thrashing around, pounding the door and shaking the door knob viciously.

"Jamie," she whispered. "Would you like to go back into your room? We'll let you go back in your room if you go to bed."

Jamie screamed and rattled the door knob again.

"Jamie, will you go to bed if we let you back in your room?"

He backed away from the door and started to cry. "Bed," he whimpered.

"Will you go back to bed?"

"Bed," he cried again.

Marianne moved to the door and called out to her husband on the other side. "Brian, Jamie says he'll go to bed if we let him back into his room. Should we try it?" She tried to inject a note of hope into her voice. The door came open a crack. Brian's tight face peered through the slit. "Jamie," he said. "Are you ready to go back to bed?"

Jamie moved eagerly toward the door. Hesitantly, Brian opened it and let him pass. Once inside, Jamie bolted toward the window.

Crying out in dismay, Brian chased him down, grabbed him by both arms and dragged him back into the hallway. Jamie kicked and howled. Brian shoved him through the doorway and pushed him to the floor.

"Brian, don't be so rough!" Marianne pleaded. "You'll hurt him."

Brian glared at her, breathing deeply and shaking his head. He wiped the back of his hand across his forehead and turned away. "Sorry," he stammered. "I guess I kind of lost it. Did I hurt him?"

Marianne helped Jamie to his feet. Shaken and frightened, the boy whimpered quietly. "It's okay, Jamie," she whispered as she rubbed the back of his head. Then she turned to her husband. "I think he's okay," she said. "Just frightened."

"Maybe this wasn't such a great idea after all," Brian muttered. He was ready to call the whole thing off. "Should we just let him go and get back to bed?" he asked.

"Let's try it once more," Marianne suggested. "We've come this far. Let's keep going a little longer and see what happens. Besides, I think Jamie has calmed down a little. Let me try talking to him again."

She turned to face her son. "Jamie, would you like to go back in your room, now? You can go back inside, but you have to get into your bed and stay there. Do you understand?"

"Bed," he said, crying softly.

"Will you go to bed, then?" Marianne repeated.

"Go." Jamie looked at his mother pleadingly.

Marianne motioned to Brian to let them pass. She led Jamie over to his bed and watched him climb inside and put his head on the pillow. She found the sheets and blankets, bunched up at the bottom of the bed, and pulled them up gently around his neck. "Good night, my Jamie," she whispered softly.

Jamie was staring up at the ceiling.

She turned to face her husband. Brian looked sick and in shock. *He's not the only one,* she thought. Jamie was back in bed, but there was little satisfaction in that achievement. The bitter taste of this night would linger for a long time.

She heard a voice, realized that Brian was speaking to her and forced herself to concentrate. "You go back into our bed, Marianne. I'll stay in here on the floor for the rest of the night. With luck, there won't be any more problems."

Nodding numbly, Marianne stumbled into her own bedroom and collapsed on the bed.

Chapter Eight
August 1991

Sara turned over on her side and tickled her younger brother in the ribs. "You little character," she teased. "What are you doing waking up so early, huh?" She tickled him again. Her jabs produced a series of loud cackles.

It was 7:20 a.m. and most of the Spencers were asleep. Not Jamie. He was still inside his sleeping bag, but he was definitely not sleeping. Something had tickled his funny bone even before his sister began tickling his ribs. He had been wiggling and giggling for ten or fifteen minutes. Sara, whose sleeping bag was next to his, had been awakened by his animated movements and sounds. Now she was making him pay for his antics.

On the other side of Sara, Angela's prostrate form lay motionless in a third sleeping bag. Older now and wiser than her sister, Angela had somehow ignored the giggles and was still fast asleep. Perhaps inspired by Angela's example, Sara stopped teasing her brother and dropped her head back on her pillow. "Okay, Jamie. Time to go back to sleep," she purred. "Isn't it fun to go camping? We can sleep as long as we want. So let's go back to sleep, now. Okay?" She turned over on her side so she was facing away from him and burrowed back inside her sleeping bag.

Jamie giggled again. He did not put his head back on his pillow or make any pretense of going back to sleep. Sara's teasing had merely added fuel to the fire; his inner spring was wound up and ticking.

On the other side of the tent trailer, Brian unzipped his sleeping bag and sat up. Slowly he looked around. Marianne lay at his side, sleeping peacefully. He had felt hot in the night and had awakened early with a burning thirst. The desire for water was not strong enough to get him out of bed, but, after overhearing the conversation on the other side of the tent, he decided he might as well get up so he could get a drink *and* rescue Sara.

Slowly he withdrew his legs, one at a time, from the sleeping bag. Then he crawled across the floor, trying to be quiet so he wouldn't wake Marianne. Parting the curtain that separated their sleeping area from the kitchen section of the little pop-up trailer, he swung his feet over the side and stood up. Now that he was outside the sleeping bag, the air felt cool, though certainly not cold. Not even at 7:30 in the morning. At least it wasn't burning hot like it had been the night before when they went to bed.

Brian tiptoed across the floor to the sink where he stopped long enough to fill up a plastic cup and drain it three times. Then he crept over to the other side of the tent where Jamie was still bouncing around. When Sara saw her father, she smiled. "Come to get Jamie?" she whispered hopefully.

Brian nodded. Sara turned gratefully over on her side again and put her head back on her pillow. Brian took Jamie by the hand. "Come on, son. Let's go see if we can find the bathroom." He helped Jamie out of his pajamas and into a T-shirt and shorts. After he had changed his own clothes, he led the boy over to the door, opened it quietly, and stepped outside.

Brian caught his breath as the brilliant hues of the landscape flooded his eyes. The night's sleep had dimmed the memory of where they were. Now he was reminded, in dramatic fashion, that they were camped in Arches National Park.

Brian took Jamie's hand and helped him down the steps of the camp trailer. Then he stopped for a moment to look around. The massive rock formations that surrounded the campsites easily captured his attention, even in the half light of early morning. Red cliffs towered above the little camp trailer like a fire engine over a lady bug. The contrast of the flame-colored rock against the rapidly bluing sky brought goose bumps to his back and neck. He stayed there by the camp trailer for awhile, trying to breathe in all the grandeur of the setting. Jamie stood silently at his side, sensing perhaps that he was in an unusual and beautiful place.

Reluctantly, Brian decided to move on. Motioning for Jamie to follow him, he stepped onto the oiled road that connected the various campsites and started walking toward the bathrooms. The eleven-year-old boy sauntered along behind him. Brian found the walk refreshing. Right now the temperature was cool and comfortable, though he knew it would warm up considerably in the next few hours. All too soon they arrived at the bathrooms. As they entered the little brick building, Brian mused over the seeming incongruity of showers in the middle of the desert. *Not exactly roughing it,* he thought.

Summer camping trips were a family tradition. They had camped at many locations in Colorado and other places in the western United States. Some had showers, some didn't. Some had no plumbing at all. He decided he liked the present arrangement just fine.

As they walked back to the trailer, Brian slowed so Jamie could catch up to him. He put his arm around the boy's shoulder as they walked together. Jamie flinched a little and bashfully tilted his head away from his father, but he didn't try to escape. He seemed unsure whether the old don't-touch-me rules applied in this new setting. Brian took advantage of the ambiguity for a rare moment of physical contact.

He glanced at Jamie out of the corner of his eye. The boy ambled along with easy flowing but somewhat awkward steps. There was something unnatural about his gait. He walked flat-footed, body tilted slightly backward, his feet reaching out like a hen's claws. The unbalanced shuffle didn't bother Brian. Jamie had always walked that way. It was part of his personality.

So was his face, a countenance as expressionless and unreadable as the rocks in the background. But it was not an ugly face, nor was there anything unnatural about it. Hazel eyes; slightly parted lips; a soft, rounded chin; and freckles — the face of universal boyhood.

Jamie's hair, tousled and uncombed, was also beautiful. The long brown locks had a soft, natural curl that Angela could not duplicate in a half-hour's work with her curling iron. Brian resisted the urge to put his hand on top of that curly head and shake it playfully. Other fathers might do that, but he knew he better not try it. Not if he wanted to preserve the present side-by-side arrangement.

As he looked at Jamie, Brian thought about the isolation and loneliness that were the boy's constant companions. He knew he didn't understand, *couldn't* understand, how the world looked through Jamie's eyes — but he *could* sense the loneliness. He wished he could penetrate that loneliness, share the burden, ease the pain — but he didn't know how to do it.

"Jamie. I love you," he said simply.

Acting on an impulse, Brian led Jamie off the road onto one of the trails that took off in every direction from the central camping area. The boy went willingly; he liked hiking. He followed his father through the rocks into a small enclosed area. On every side tall cliffs rose from the valley floor like the walls of a fortress. The tops of the cliffs blazed with fire from the morning sun, though the valley was still shrouded in shadow. Underneath, the soil was red and dusty. A few scraggly bushes clung precariously to cracks in the rugged walls, and here and there a clump of grass or wild flowers bloomed at the edge of the sandy trail.

Brian put his hand on the solid wall and felt the gritty texture of the sandstone with his fingers. He put his other arm around Jamie's shoulder and pulled him closer. Passive and subdued, Jamie submitted to his father's touch, gazing reverently with him at the majestic rocks that surrounded them. For a few moments, the boy stood with the man, reconciled through the mediating power of nature, joined in a silent bond that temporarily transcended the vast gulf between them.

It was a moment Brian would remember for the rest of his life. He stayed there as long as he dared, one arm around his son and the other reaching out to the empowering walls of the canyon. Then, reluctantly, he pulled his arm away from Jamie's shoulder and nudged him gently back down the path to the campground.

◆◆◆

"Anyone ready for a hike?" It was Marianne who posed the question, and it was she who made the first move to disperse the breakfast inertia that held them bound. Brian, Angela, Sara, and Jamie were lounging around the tent and picnic table in various stages of inactivity. Nor did anyone respond immediately to Marianne's invitation. So she prodded. First her husband. Then the girls.

"Come on," she urged as she poked and tickled her reticent companions. "Let's go see what all these rocks do for a living."

Angela's expression communicated more clearly than words that rocks came pretty far down on her list of favorite things. Nevertheless, she arose with a sigh and took off in the general direction of the van. One by one, the others followed. Jamie, always an advocate for outdoor exploring, showed the most enthusiasm.

Once up, Brian walked slowly to his position in the driver's seat of the van. Sensing that his hesitation was mostly teasing, Marianne gave him an extra poke as he stepped up into the van. As soon as everyone was inside, Brian started the engine and drove slowly through the campground area to the junction of the main highway through the park. "Which way?" he asked as the van pulled up to the stop sign.

Marianne was looking at a map. "Shall we go to Landscape Arch or Delicate Arch, or where?" she asked.

"What's the one you see on Utah license plates?"

"I think that's Delicate Arch," she replied. "It's one of the more spectacular ones. And it looks like you have to hike a ways to get to it."

"Let's go there," Brian suggested.

Marianne turned around to the others. "Is it okay if we go to Delicate Arch? Is that all right with you guys?"

"Whatever," said Sara. "You decide, mom."

Marianne looked at Brian again and pointed to the left. He turned onto the highway and began following the signs to Delicate Arch. As they sped across the arid landscape, the family showed signs of increasing interest and excitement. From time to time they peeked out the windows to capture the unusual shapes and colors that flashed by. With a little imagination they could easily turn the rocks into sculptures. One rock looked like a rusty army tank; another was shaped like a ballet dancer. One particularly long formation was described in the park brochure as a parade of elephants.

After they had traveled a few miles, a large brown sign marked the turnoff to Delicate Arch. Brian followed the pointing arrow. At this early hour, traffic was still light. However, there were several cars in the parking lot when they arrived at the trail head. Marianne opened her door and jumped down to the ground. The others grabbed hats and followed her to the beginning of the trail. The bright sunshine, not yet uncomfortably hot, made their surroundings seem pleasant and inviting. They were smiling and laughing now. Marianne felt unusually cheerful as she started out with her family on the path to Delicate Arch.

For a while they walked on level ground. Hiking slowly and leisurely, they surveyed the nearby rock formations, searching for arches. They had seen several of the unusual structures since arriving in the park the previous evening, but always at a distance. Now they had a close-up view. Some of the arches cut part way through the stone; others were complete holes that revealed blue sky on the other side. Most of the arches were small, but some were large enough that it would be scary to stand on top of them.

Even Angela's curiosity had been sparked. "Dad, what makes these arches?" she asked. "And why are there so many of them here in this one place?"

Brian thought for a minute. "Well, I'm no geologist and I'm not sure I understand it very well myself. I think it's because the layers of rock on top are harder than those underneath. When the wind blows and the rain comes down, it wears away the part underneath faster than the part on top. So you get a hole in the rock, and then an arch or even a bridge." It wasn't a fancy explanation, but it seemed to satisfy Angela's curiosity. They hiked on in silence.

After a while the trail began to climb. They were moving up the face of a huge stone mountain. No path was discernible on the hard rocky surface; painted arrows directed them as they climbed. It was definitely hotter now. Soon everyone was puffing and gasping for breath. They stopped and sat down on the rock to rest for a few minutes. Then they got up and began plodding along again.

At one point the trail veered left into a small canyon, with rock walls on both sides. They walked in single file, without conversation—each focused on the immediate task of putting one foot in front of another along the hot, dusty trail. Unexpectedly, the path emerged from the canyon and turned sharply to the right along the rock face. At the edge of the trail a steep slope plunged into a deep gorge. There was no railing— just a sudden drop into space. Marianne sucked in her breath and stepped back.

Then she saw Jamie.

He was right in front of her, shuffling along the trail. He seemed unaware of the drop off at his left. Alarmed, Marianne moved quickly up beside him and grabbed his hand. Instantly, he stiffened and pulled away. She shifted her grip to his arm and held on tight.

Jamie squealed and tried to free his arm. He started to squirm and wiggle. Marianne's heart froze inside her. What if he struggled harder and she couldn't hold him? He might fall over the edge of the cliff . . . and maybe pull her with him! She looked around for Brian, but he was somewhere behind her and had not yet emerged from the canyon. Muscles tensing involuntarily, she tried to push Jamie up against the inside wall of the trail. She felt his body retaliate, pushing against her. He was stronger than she remembered, and his struggles were intensifying. She was losing control and she knew it. A rush of panic surged through her body. A scream formed in her chest and was almost into her mouth when she heard a voice in the back of her mind.

Marianne, it said. *Let go.* It was a quiet voice, and in response she relaxed her body for just an instant. Then she felt Jamie's convulsive movements and the panic returned. She couldn't let go of Jamie. He didn't recognize the danger. He just might walk right over the edge of the cliff.

Marianne, let go! The voice was stronger now. It forced her head up and brought reason back into her mind. Somehow, it made more sense than her other panicky thoughts. Better not to overreact. Play it cool and things would turn out okay. Keep struggling and it could get away from her.

Taking a deep breath, she stepped back and released her grip on Jamie's arm. She stayed between him and the edge of the cliff, ready to tackle him if he moved in that direction. He jerked away, rubbing his arm like he had just brushed away a stinging insect. He watched his mother cautiously as if afraid she might come after him again. Then, just as his father emerged from the gap behind, Jamie turned and began marching once more along the trail. Marianne followed, watching every move with a tight feeling in her chest. Her legs felt weak and wobbly. But she was thankful to be out of that terrifying situation.

A few minutes later the little company reached the end of the trail and came out on top of the stone mountain. Beneath them stood Delicate Arch. Gigantic and imposing, it framed a picture book landscape of desert rocks and distant mountains. Veins of orange, white, and chocolate-colored rock ran horizontally through the columns of the arch, appearing again as a reflection in the surrounding formations. The columns of the arch were thick and stocky at the base and on the top, thinner in the middle; one place on the left side looked dangerously thin, giving the impression that the whole structure might collapse at any moment. The overall effect of Delicate Arch was enhanced by its isolation. Alone in the middle of a solid sea of rock, it cut into the sky like a massive doughnut standing edgewise on the broad plateau.

Marianne stared wordlessly at this masterpiece of mother nature's artwork. It was beautiful. Beautiful enough—perhaps—to justify the price she had paid to see it.

◆ ◆ ◆

Brian had volunteered to fix dinner on the second day of the trip. Not known for his cooking ability, he had nevertheless been planning this one for weeks—his Dutch oven dinner.

He started early, well before 5:00. The sun was mercilessly hot at that hour, even in the shade of the juniper tree that partially shielded their picnic table. Ignoring the heat, Brian started a fire in the pit, feeding it with larger and larger pieces of wood until it was a roaring blaze. Then he added half a bag of charcoal.

With the fire underway, Brian gathered everything he would need from the camp trailer and carried it to the picnic table. Lifting the heavy iron Dutch oven onto the table, he wiped it out carefully with a piece of paper towel and lined it with aluminum foil. He reached for the package of chicken breasts and peeled off the butcher paper. The pieces of meat were still partially frozen and stuck together, so he pried them apart. Then he went back into the trailer, lit one of the burners on the stove, and placed the chicken breasts in a pan over the flame.

While the chicken was browning, Brian opened a can of cream of mushroom soup and a can of cream of celery soup and poured them into the Dutch oven. Then he opened a package of rice and measured out two cups. So far so good. This was pretty simple. That's what he liked about Dutch oven cooking. It was easy to do, and everything always tasted so good.

As soon as the chicken was partially cooked, he carried the frying pan outside and put it on the table by the Dutch oven. With a fork he speared the pieces of meat and gently dropped them into the soupy mixture, noting each plop with satisfaction. He seasoned his Dutch oven dinner with salt and pepper and onion salt and replaced the lid. Lifting the black kettle by its long wiry handle, he carried it over to the fire. With a stick he spread the logs apart and set the Dutch oven on a bed of red-hot coals in the center of the fire. Then he shoveled more burning logs and pieces of charcoal on top of the big kettle.

With the main dish steaming in the fire, Brian carved a cantaloupe and got out the dishes and silverware. He opened a can of green beans and put them in a small pot on the stove. Then he sat down to wait.

During all these preparations Marianne had been reading a book in a lawn chair under the juniper tree. Happy to have someone else doing the cooking, she had purposely stayed out of Brian's way. But thirty minutes into the cook-out, she made an observation.

"That looks pretty hot there in the middle of the fire, honey. Do you think it will get done too much?"

"Well, it's supposed to take forty minutes. There's still ten to go."

"Maybe you should check it," she suggested diplomatically. "I don't know if it's good to have a hot fire burning around the Dutch oven like that. Aren't you supposed to just use coals?"

"I don't think it matters too much what you use," he answered stiffly.

"Okay," Marianne replied with a little too much certainty, and returned to her book.

Fact: Brian's Dutch oven cooking expertise was mostly in his head; the Dutch oven was a new addition to their camping equipment and today's meal marked his maiden voyage in open-fire cooking. He had researched the topic and talked to others who were more knowledgeable, but he remained sadly lacking in experience. Maybe that's why Marianne's comment made him uneasy. In any case, after another minute or two had passed, he decided to take a look inside the Dutch oven. He used a claw hammer to lift it out of the fire. Then he removed the lid with the same tool and peeked inside.

It was not a pretty sight.

The center of the pot was still soupy — not liquid any more, but too gooey to eat with a fork. Around the edge was a solid crust about a quarter of an inch thick. The crust was black. The entire mixture bubbled vigorously.

Brian's chin dropped faster than a nine-iron chip shot when he saw the stuff in the Dutch oven. Seizing a large wooden spoon, he jabbed it into the pot and began to stir, hoping to even things out a bit. Instead, he succeeded in dislodging little chunks of the burnt crust and spreading them throughout the casserole. He stopped stirring. Then he gave a big sigh. Trembling, he scooped up a spoonful of rice and chewed on it. It tasted different than he had expected. Sort of crunchy and scorched at the same time. He poked a fork into a chicken breast and stripped off a little piece to taste it. It tasted a bit flat, but at least it was done.

He decided to lower his expectations. While his special dish didn't look or taste quite the way he had anticipated, it might suffice to feed some hungry people. Cooking it longer didn't seem advisable. Might as well go for it. So he picked up the Dutch oven and carried it over to the picnic table. He took off the lid again and stirred the burnt-on-the-outside gooey-on-the-inside stuff one last time. He put the vegetable and fruit alongside the main dish. Then he looked up and smiled. "Anyone hungry?" he asked cheerfully.

The other members of the family scrambled eagerly over to the table and stuck out their plates. Brian dished out generous portions to everyone and pretended not to notice the looks on their faces when they saw the lumpy stew with the little black flakes in it. They found places to sit at the picnic table and cautiously tested a few mouthfuls of dad's Dutch oven delight. That's as far as Angela and Sara got, though they did pick at the chicken. Marianne ate her portion dutifully and made some comment about how good things tasted when they were cooked in the great outdoors.

Jamie came back for seconds.

After Brian had finished his own plate of food, he sat thoughtfully for a few minutes. Finally he cleared his throat and turned to face his wife.

"Should I try the cobbler?" Something in his voice suggested that he was leaning toward a *no* answer.

"Go for it," she whispered.

Brian got up slowly from the table and went back over to the Dutch oven. He stopped and stared at it for quite a few seconds, like a soldier checking out a land mine to see if it had been deactivated. Finally he stepped forward. Finding a large bowl, he scooped out the remaining contents, removed the aluminum foil, and stuck the big kettle back into the fire. Then he returned to the trailer and searched through the sack of dry goods. After poking around for a few minutes, he found what he was looking for—a yellow cake mix, a can of sweetened blueberry filling, and two cans of Sprite. He smiled. This time he would do it right.

Returning to the fire, he extracted the Dutch oven again, opened it and scraped out the charred remnants of the casserole. He opened the can of blueberries and dumped them into the pot. Then he poured the cake mix on top and closed the lid again. This part was so easy.

Back to the fire. Once again he placed the Dutch oven on a bed of coals. He shoveled a few coals on top, but this time he was careful to push the two branches that still sprouted flames away from the kettle. He stayed by the fire, checking his watch every few minutes. After twenty minutes he pulled the Dutch oven from the fire and looked inside. No black in there. At thirty minutes he lifted the lid off again and poured the two cans of *Sprite* on top of the cake. Then, at thirty-five minutes he checked it once more. The cake was solid and brown on top. Just right. He lifted the big pot from the fire, carried it over to the table, and invited everyone to come for dessert.

No one declined the Dutch oven dessert, though Angela mumbled something about preferring chocolate. Jamie came back three times. Each time he held out his plate and said "mo cake." The third time Brian dished up just one spoonful for him because the dessert was so sweet. But the cook ate two and a half portions himself. He felt a whole lot better about his cooking after it was all done.

After dinner, Angela and Sara washed the dishes while Brian cleaned out the Dutch oven and put it back into the fire. Since it was not yet dark, Marianne suggested another walk before bedtime. The girls declined, opting to play a game on the picnic table. Marianne changed her mind about the walk; instead, she moved her lawn chair over by the fire and sat down. After a while Brian joined her. They sat by the fire for a while without speaking, enjoying the solitude.

Later, Brian took Jamie to the bathroom again and helped him get on his pajamas. "Did you have fun today, Jamie?" he inquired as the boy was pulling on his pajama top.

"Fun today," said Jamie.

"Did you like the hike?"

Brian got no answer to that one. So he helped Jamie into his sleeping bag and went back outside. The girls were still playing cards. It was getting dark now, so the card game took place in the light of a large electric lantern. Insects, some of them very large, buzzed around the lantern and crawled on the table. The girls didn't seem to notice. They were laughing and giggling. Brian watched them for awhile. Then he made his way back over to the fire, where Marianne sat watching the flames.

"Tired?" he asked as he pulled up another chair.

She looked up and smiled. "A little, I guess. I'm not used to all this outdoor activity. It's been fun, though. Except for that scary moment on the Delicate Arch trail."

"What scary moment was that?"

"I guess I didn't tell you about it, did I? Well, it was when we were on that section of the trail with the big drop off. Do you remember that part?"

"I think so."

Marianne tried to remember the details. "I got there first with Jamie," she said. "You were still back on the trail behind us. When I saw that cliff, I got worried. I had horrible visions of Jamie stepping nonchalantly off the ledge and falling to his death. But when I tried to take his hand, he balked and made a fuss. Then I got really panicky because I thought he might fight against me and drag both of us over the edge. Finally I decided it was better to step back and not make a big deal about it. When I did that he calmed down and made it just fine. I was sure nervous. But, you know, I think I learned something important from that experience."

"What did you learn, Marianne?" Brian poked at the fire with a stick.

"I learned that things go better with Jamie if I just relax, accept him as he is, and don't worry so much about him. I realized today that he really is a person—not just a project. The quality of his life is not the same as ours. He's different in so many ways. But . . . how can I say this? The similarities outweigh the differences. I think I have focused too much on the differences. I want to see him more as a person. I want to appreciate him for what he is." She paused for a moment, then continued tentatively: "I don't know if I'm making any sense."

"You're making a lot of sense."

"It's funny. I don't expect as much anymore. Maybe if I expect less, I'll get more." Marianne's voice trailed off momentarily as she stared at the fire. She picked up a twig from the ground, snapped it in two, and dropped it into the flames. Then she stood up and turned her back to the fire. Slowly, emphatically, she spoke again.

"There's something else, Brian. You know, I have the feeling that there's more to Jamie than we see. We don't know who he really is. He's like a horse with hobbles on its legs. But the hobbles are not really part of him. They're kind of a temporary restraint. Someday, when those hobbles come off, we'll find out that he's just like the rest of us."

"What if the hobbles don't come off?" Brian interjected softly. "I know we need to keep hoping for something that will make him normal, but realistically . . ."

"I'm not talking about that," Marianne interrupted, shaking her head. "I've accepted the fact that Jamie will never be whole in this life." Her voice was husky. "Brian," she said, with an intensity that brought his head up quickly to meet her eyes, "If there's a heaven, and if I ever get there, I just know I'll find Jamie there, too. Then he and I will sit down and have a long talk. He'll tell me what it was like to live with us: what he learned; how he felt; what was going through his mind all those times when nothing came out of his mouth. And then I'll find out . . . I'll find out who he really is."

Marianne searched her husband's eyes one last time. Then she turned her face toward the fire. Brian got up from his chair, moved over beside her, and put his arm around her waist. After a while, when the light from the fire had grown dim and the stars were bright overhead, they turned away from the fire and walked hand in hand back to the camp trailer.

Chapter Nine
June 1993

"Jamie? A boy scout?"

Marianne gave her husband a puzzled look. His suggestion had caught her completely by surprise. It was the last thing she expected to hear on their after-dinner walk around the neighborhood.

"Sure," Brian replied. "Jamie's thirteen years old now. And you know how he loves to camp. I know he won't be able to do merit badges or anything like that, but he could go on some of the activities. Now that I'm a scoutmaster, I thought it would be fun to have my own son come along."

Marianne stopped to admire a honeysuckle that draped the fence along the sidewalk. Leaves and tendrils sprouted profusely along the entire length of the fence, creating a spongy green mattress that looked soft enough to push on its side and lie down on. As she reached out to touch the luxuriant vegetation, Marianne was thinking about the scout thing. She had a concern.

"Don't you think it might, uh, disrupt the scout troop to have Jamie there?" she asked. "I mean, what will the other boys think of him?" She stepped back from the honeysuckle and started walking again. "Brian, boys that age can be very unkind. What if . . . what if they make fun of him and tease him?"

"I suppose that's always a possibility." Brian cleared his throat. "But I like the boys in this troop. They're good kids. With a little encouragement, I think some of them might even take Jamie under their wing and stick up for him. Anyway, we need to try. We can't protect him all his life. Besides, how is this different from going to school? Jamie does okay in school, doesn't he?"

"He does do pretty well in school," Marianne admitted. "That's what his teachers say, anyway. However, I did find out a few weeks ago that he gets teased sometimes. Did you know that they have a nickname for him?"

"A nickname?"

"Yes. Mrs. Crockett told me about it just before school let out for the summer. Apparently, some of the kids call him Klutzie — Klutzie Spencer." Marianne pronounced the word like the name of a loathsome disease. "And I guess they do make fun of him. I'm not sure exactly how many kids are involved or what they do — I don't think it's widespread. I guess you have to expect some of that in seventh grade. But most of the kids seem to treat him well."

"That sounds like junior high school, all right," Brian commented. "And high school. I've heard lots of names over the years. Been called a few myself."

"Overall, I'd have to say that Jamie does pretty well at school," Marianne continued. "Whenever I've seen him there he's just sitting quietly and watching what's going on. Of course he doesn't understand everything, and he doesn't say much, but he doesn't cause problems, either — unless he gets upset about something. Still . . . school's different. They're prepared to deal with him in his special ed. class. But a scout troop?" She shook her head as she tried to imagine Jamie wearing a boy scout uniform.

"Maybe Jamie would be one of the best behaved boys in the scout troop, too," Brian suggested. "It might be nice to have a quiet kid in that bunch." He took Marianne's hand, interlocking his fingers with hers. His face took on a determined profile. "You know, Marianne," he said firmly, "I think Jamie can handle it."

She looked at him, met his eyes with her own. Finally she nodded and said, "Okay. I'll go along with you. Let's give it a try." Playfully, she tossed her head from side to side. "Jamie, the boy scout," she sang softly to herself. "Even has a nice ring to it." She smiled at Brian.

After that they walked along in silence for awhile. The evening breeze from the canyon cooled their faces and soothed their senses. Marianne tried to relax and let her mind wander for awhile. Eventually, as so often happened, it came back to her children.

"I had a little talk with Sara this morning," she remarked to Brian. "Do you want to know what her latest plans are?"

"Sure," he replied with a grin. "Let me guess." He pursed his lips and rolled his eyes as if trying to solve a tough riddle. "She's decided not to go to college in the fall," he quipped. "She's going to spend a month touring Europe instead. Right?"

Marianne burst out laughing as the image of her daughter jaunting across Europe evoked an all-too-plausible scenario. But she shook her finger at Brian. "Nice guess," she retorted. "But I'm afraid you're wrong this time. It's not *that* dramatic. Sara's plans for another year of college haven't changed — not yet, anyway. But it looks like she won't be living at home like we thought."

"So she wants to move out, huh? Into an apartment?"

Marianne nodded. "Says she needs to get out on her own."

"Does she have some place in mind?"

"Montebello Apartments. She wants to room with a friend — a girl she met in her orchestra class last year. They roomed together on the tour. If this other girl likes to play as much as Sara, it should be quite a swinging apartment."

"That's our Sara, all right," Brian agreed. H shook his head. "You know, I don't think I've ever met anyone who makes friends as fast as she does. I remember taking her to the park once when she was about ten years old. There was another little girl playing on the swings. In five minutes she and Sara were fast friends—running around the playground together, going up and down the slide—you name it." Brian paused for a moment, then continued: "Moving out in her sophomore year." He seemed to be thinking it through. "Can she afford it?"

"That's what I asked. She says she will have enough money. She has her job in the bookstore. She seems to think she'll be able to get by okay as long as she keeps working."

"Well, I guess it's up to her. I'd feel better if she lived at home for another year, though." He shook his head again. "Why do they grow up so fast, anyway?"

It was a rhetorical question, but Marianne answered it anyway. "I don't know why they grow up so fast," she sighed, "but they do." She paused for a moment, then continued philosophically, "Oh, well, it's not all bad. You know, it's been nice to have Angie finally become an adult. I miss having her home, but when she does come around, it's different than it used to be. None of that mother-daughter thing that used to get in the way. It's like we're really friends, now. I like it."

"Have you seen her recently?"

"Yes. As a matter of fact, she stopped in today to get some more of her clothes. We had a nice talk about Nate."

"Nate?" he said. "Who's Nate? Have I met him?"

"Yes, you have. He's the guy she's been dating—the one who came to the barbecue at our house on Memorial Day. Remember?"

"Oh, yeah. *That* Nate. I thought she broke up with that guy."

"She did—for a couple of weeks. But now they're back together again, and, according to Angie, things are better than ever."

"Good. He seemed like a nice guy." Brian's voice trailed off momentarily. Then all at once he turned back to Marianne. "Hey. Are you trying to tell me something?" he demanded. "Is this thing with Angie and Nate getting serious?"

"I don't think so," she answered, smiling at his hasty conclusion. "Angie says she's not ready to settle down yet. But one of these times . . ." Her voice turned soft and for a moment there was a wistful look in her eyes.

Brian's voice brought her back to the present. "Did Angie say anything about her new job?" he inquired. "Are they keeping her busy at US West?"

"Well, I don't know. She likes what she's doing, but it's quite different from being a student. Now that she's graduated from college and there's only work to worry about, I think it's taking some time for her to adjust. In fact, she told me today that she doesn't have enough to do this summer. Says she's bored. Imagine that."

Brian smiled, amused perhaps at the idea of his oldest daughter's being bored. Then his face became serious. "I guess that's one of Jamie's challenges, too," he said. "It's hard to find things for him to do sometimes, isn't it?"

Marianne nodded. "Definitely. Jamie doesn't have enough to do, especially during the summer. He spends much of the day just sitting on his bed. Or he paces around the house. He opens the doors to look outside but rarely goes out into the yard. I've been trying to do some things with him, like playing games and reading to him. But it's so hard to keep him busy."

"Yeah, I know what you mean," said Brian. "It's hard for me to think of things to do with him, too. Guess I'm not very creative when it comes to that." He paused for a moment, then seemed to reconsider. "On the other hand," he continued, "Jamie and I have done a few things together—like jumping on the trampoline after dinner. He seems to like that. And sometimes he'll throw a ball back and forth a few times. It's not much, but every little bit helps."

"You're right," she agreed. "Every little bit of progress is important." Marianne remembered something else that Jamie had done recently—an achievement of sorts. She wanted to tell Brian about it. But they were getting close to their street; the walk was almost over. Taking Brian by the hand, she led him over to the edge of the sidewalk, sat down on the curb, and pulled him down beside her. She made herself as comfortable as possible. Then she turned to Brian.

"Jamie has come a long way from where he was a few years ago," she said. "When you were talking about the trampoline, it reminded me of something that's happened recently that's kind of encouraging. I don't know if you've noticed it or not."

"What's happened is that Jamie's developed an interest in music. A few weeks ago, after I had been listening to a Carpenters CD, he came up to me and said, "Moosic on." It took me a while to figure out what he was talking about. Finally I played that album again for him. He sat down on the couch and listened to the whole thing. I couldn't believe it. Since then he's done the same thing with two or three other CDs. He will sit attentively for an hour or longer when he listens to music. And I can tell he's really into it, feeling it. Sometimes he rocks back and forth to the music. Sometimes he even tries to sing along." Marianne stopped talking and her eyes grew misty as she pictured her Jamie sitting on the couch listening to her music.

"That's neat, Marianne," Brian offered. "I'd like to see him doing that." Marianne nodded without speaking. After that, both of them were silent for awhile.

Brian was the first to move. Leaning back, he put both hands on the sidewalk behind him and propped himself up. Slowly he looked around—at the vacant lawns, the secluded trees, the deserted sidewalk. Then he looked at his wife, studying her carefully. "We could use a little of that music ourselves, right about now," he suggested.

Marianne turned to him with a puzzled look on her face. "What?" she asked. "What are you talking about?" Then she saw the look in his eyes. "Brian," she scolded, shaking her head. "Honestly, sometimes you get romantic at the strangest times." She jabbed him on the arm and pushed him away. But she wasn't frowning.

Brian leaned over and put his arm around her shoulders. "Sorry," he whispered in her ear. "I think it's the setting. I've never kissed a girl in the gutter before." Both of them laughed. Then he turned her face toward him and kissed her softly on the mouth.

Marianne felt herself sinking into his embrace. She forgot about Jamie and Angela and Sara and boy scouts and everything else. For a moment, she sat wordlessly next to Brian, enjoying the warmth and security he provided. Then she stood up and pulled him to his feet. She gave him another quick kiss on the cheek and they started walking again.

Two minutes later they were rounding the corner into their cul-de-sac; the house was just half a block away. It was nearly 9:00 p.m. and darkness was finally creeping into the mid-summer evening. They sauntered leisurely down the sidewalk in the gathering dusk, savoring a few final moments in the cool outside air. At the front door of the house, they stopped for a final embrace. Then Brian opened the door for his wife and together they stepped back into the real world.

◆◆◆

"Pretty," the boy said to himself. He held the pretty thing up in front of his face and wiggled his hand to make it move around. He chuckled as he watched it dance in front of his eyes. He thought it was very beautiful.

Jamie cradled the pretty thing in his hand. He touched the front of it with his thumb and rubbed it between his fingers. He put his hand all the way around it and held it tight. Then he pulled his fist up next to his face and rubbed it gently across his cheek. It felt good to hold the pretty thing in his hand. He held it for a long time, looking at it and feeling it with his fingers.

Jamie thought about the pretty thing. Something was wrong with it. It was broken. It didn't do anything or say anything, and nobody used it. It was always by itself. Always alone. He felt sad when he thought about the pretty thing being broken. He opened his hand so he could see it again. He rubbed it gently. "Broken," he said to the pretty thing. Then he started to cry.

After a while Jamie stopped crying. He felt a little better. He thought about the pretty thing and how much he liked it. He remembered how good he felt when he looked at it and when he touched it. He held it up in front of his face and rubbed it again with his fingers. "Pretty," he said, talking to the object in his hand. "Pretty," he repeated. Then he smiled.

Jamie smiled at the gold watch.

◆◆◆

Sara was sprawled out on her bed reading a book when her father poked his head through the door.

"I hear you're moving out," he remarked casually. "It's gonna be pretty quiet around here without Sara to keep things stirred up."

"Yup," she said without looking up from her book. "But I'm not going for awhile. Not until the end of August. So don't count on peace and quiet just yet. Okay?"

"Okay. I won't panic just yet." Brian lifted his head a little higher so he could see over the top of the book. "Have you figured out how you're going to get around next year without a car?" he asked.

The book came down. "Actually, dad," Sara mumbled, "I'm not exactly sure what to do about that. It's too far to walk to school. I don't have enough money to buy a car. I was kind of hoping that one of my roommates would have a car, or something."

"Sounds kind of iffy to me."

"I know. But something will turn up. I'm not going to worry about it."

"Okay. I won't worry about it either." Brian pulled his head back through the doorway and went upstairs.

When he went into the bedroom to take off his shoes, Brian found Jamie sitting on the edge of the bed. Jamie had his pajamas on and should have been in his own bed at that hour. Brian's first inclination was to send his son back to his own room. Then he saw something that made him stop and wait.

Jamie was playing with the gold pocket watch.

There was something unusual about the situation. In contrast to the carry-around toys that he shook and flipped and dropped, Jamie held this object securely in the palm of his hand, gently rubbing the gold case with his fingers. As he caressed the watch, he smiled and spoke soft words that Brian could not hear. His voice was low and musical.

He's talking to the watch, Brian realized. Yes, Jamie was speaking to the gold watch, even as a widow might talk to a picture of her departed husband. The boy had always clung to objects like Linus to his security blanket, but Brian had never seen this kind of personification before; the intimacy surpassed any human interaction with Jamie that Brian could remember. Reluctant to interrupt, he stayed outside the room and watched unobtrusively through the door. Somehow he was not worried that Jamie would lose or damage the watch. It almost seemed that the old timepiece belonged to *him*.

Time stood still for Jamie. The boy was in no hurry. So Brian watched and waited for quite a while. Only after he sensed that the ritual was winding down did Brian enter the room and sit down on the bed by his son. "Hi, Jamie," he said. "That's a beautiful watch, isn't it? Do you like it, Jamie?"

"Like it Jamie," said the boy, still clutching the shiny object.

"It's time to go to bed now, Jamie. Come on. I'll help you into your bed." Brian took Jamie by the hand and gently pulled him to his feet. Together they walked down the hallway and into the boy's bedroom. Jamie got into bed and allowed his father to pull the covers over him. "Good night, son," said Brian. Then he reached down and slipped the pocket watch out of the boy's hand and into his own. Jamie watched as his father got slowly to his feet and walked out of the room.

Brian went back into his own bedroom and sat down at the desk. He lifted up the old timepiece to look at it, holding the long stem with his fingers so that the watch dangled in the palm of his hand.

He hadn't looked at the watch for years. But now he examined it with renewed interest. Though the timepiece made no sound, he couldn't resist looking at the hands to see if their position had changed. 12:27. Not a minute more or less than before.

How long had it been 12:27?

He wondered what the world had been like when the hands of the watch were in motion— when his father carried the timepiece in his vest pocket, when his grandfather took it with him to the ball. What unusual events from past generations had that mute face witnessed? He wished the watch could talk and reveal its lifetime secrets.

Then he had a revelation. This watch did not belong in *his* generation. Even if it were working, its intricate elegance would be out of place in a world of digital clocks and five-function wrist watches. For a moment he felt sorry for the old timepiece.

Brian put the gold watch on the desk in front of him and studied it thoughtfully. So beautiful. So exquisitely crafted. Was that why Jamie was attracted to it? The ancient timepiece might be nonfunctional and out of place, but there was a timeless, eternal quality about it that made it worthy of admiration and respect.

Reverently, Brian cradled the gold watch once again in his hand and then gently put it back in its accustomed place on the desk.

Chapter Ten
August 1993

In a remote part of the Rocky Mountains west of Colorado Springs, a narrow column of men and boys inched its way up a steep hill. They were hiking in a wilderness area populated with trees, ground cover, and wildlife. Tall, woody pines with gnarly arms and leafy hands shut out the light from the mid-morning sun overhead. Underneath, the grassy hillside bristled with logs and sticks in various stages of decay.

Occasionally a branch cracked underfoot as a boy accidentally—or deliberately—stepped on it. The boisterous noises and chattering voices of the humans seemed out of place in a setting that for millennia had echoed only to the songs of birds, the buzzing of insects, and the rustling sounds of small animals. The very presence of the hikers in the forest seemed intrusive.

Near the back of the column a small figure marched along as silently as the hidden animals in the forest. His movements contrasted with those of the other boys in the party. Tiptoeing through the trees in his awkward, uneven gait, he peered anxiously in every direction, perhaps partly in fear of some lurking animal and partly in fascination at the strange new world around him.

A man walked at the boy's side, keeping a watchful eye on him and occasionally checking on the other boys as well. At the other end of the column a second adult marched with the youngsters. Altogether, two men and seven boys. The boy on the end was James Spencer. He was one of them—one of the boy scouts.

If he didn't understand exactly what a boy scout was, Jamie nevertheless *looked* like a boy scout. He looked great in his new scout uniform. He liked the shirt with the patch on the left shoulder that read "328." He was wearing the shirt now, with a pair of matching green shorts. His neckerchief was red and blue and fastened with a silver clasp molded to look like a coiled rope. On his back was a small, light backpack to carry his lunch and an extra pair of socks. He even had his own hiking shoes, low cut but sturdy and firm on the sides, with corrugated soles that provided a firm footing on the soft crumbly soil of the forest.

At his side, his father turned his head again to monitor Jamie's progress. "Do you like the hike, Jamie?" he asked.

"Hike," said the boy. The response was terse, but the smile that accompanied it conveyed a lot of information.

The boy scout on the other side of Jamie's father chimed into the conversation. "Yeah, Jamie. This is great, huh? You like being a scout?" There was no response to these questions, but Jeremy kept talking anyway. "Pretty soon we'll be over this hill. Then we'll be at the lake. The lake will be lots of fun, Jamie."

Brian listened idly to the one-sided conversation. Cocking his head again to look at Jamie, he tried to assess the impact of Jeremy's words. On a scale of increasing responsiveness from one to ten, Jamie's reaction was pretty close to a one. Ignoring the attention from the other boy, Jamie continued to scan the forest for whatever he was looking for.

Brian smiled to himself. Putting the reticent boy into an adventuresome situation with new companions hadn't transformed him into a talking wonder. That was okay. Brian wasn't expecting any miracles. He was content to have his son along on this hiking trip. Jamie was bound to learn something from this experience.

Brian turned his eyes away from his son to survey the forest around them. There was something magical about this place; the warmth of the sun, the coolness of the shadows, the aroma of the earth, the sights and sounds of nature were a soothing potion. Brian took a deep breath and felt the air flow into his lungs and surge through his body. The forest was therapeutic, and he was feeling high. He felt like a William Wordsworth who could write poetry about being in such a place on such a day.

But the poetry would have to wait. There were other, more practical matters demanding his attention. Reluctantly, Brian pulled his eyes away from the magical terrain of the forest and focused straight ahead. He figured they were almost to the top of the hill. The trail they were following was faint and apparently used infrequently; when they got to the top they would leave it altogether. Then, if the map they had acquired from the Forest Service was accurate, there was a good-sized lake off to the left just over the top of the rise. They would stop at the lake to play, eat lunch, work on some outdoor skills, and then start back. None of them had brought fishing gear, so there would be no fishing on this trip.

Kelly, the oldest of the boys at fourteen, saw the top of the rise and broke into a sprint. He was the first to go over the top. The other boys hooted and hurried after him, except for Jamie, who stayed back with his father. As the men and boys reached level ground and turned to the left, they were greeted by a view of more of the forest. No water, just trees. The boys moaned in disappointment. But Chad Livingston, the assistant scoutmaster, motioned for them to turn off the trail and keep marching. "It's down that way, guys," he barked in a drill sergeant-like voice. The boys turned in the direction he had pointed and resumed their hike.

Brian had met Chad Livingston just four months earlier when they both signed up with the same scout troop. Chad was smaller than Brian, but no less athletic. He had just the right build for crossing deserts and climbing mountains. His most distinctive feature was a full-face beard, neatly trimmed and black except for a few gray hairs. Like Brian, he wore the traditional green scout uniform, but on his head was a bright orange baseball cap that served the dual purpose of stylizing his uniform and covering his balding head.

Chad was an outdoorsman from head to toe. A car salesman by profession, he lived for fishing season and the deer hunt. He and his wife spent much of their summers in the mountains, living out of their camper truck. Chad was ten to fifteen years older than Brian. He'd been in Boy Scouting for over twenty years and had given service at many different levels. He was comfortable with the program and confident in his knowledge and experience. Occasionally, his exuberance for nature and discipline overshadowed his sensitivity to the needs and feelings of the boys. He was a strict taskmaster. But it was a minor fault, and easily forgiven in light of his firm commitment and eagerness to help. Brian was relatively new to scouting, and he was glad to have Chad Livingston around to share his knowledge and experience with the boys.

At the moment, Chad looked cool and rested. Brian, however, was beginning to feel the effects of the long climb. Out of shape, he wheezed to himself. They had been hiking for almost an hour. He felt his heart pounding and noticed that he was breathing hard in the thin mountain air. He slowed his pace a bit. Thankfully, the others matched his stride. Brian began searching the forest floor for a good walking stick. He spotted one right away, a long straight branch with a knob on one end. Without breaking stride, he scooped it up, broke off the pointed end, and began to lean on it with each step. After five minutes, he wasn't sure it was helping that much, but it made him feel more like a real mountaineer.

Then he noticed something that he had not anticipated.

At his side, Jamie was tramping along with his very own walking stick. Smaller, and not quite as straight as his father's, it was nevertheless clearly the same type of device. With each step, Jamie poked the ground ahead with the stick. He hadn't quite captured the idea of using it to support his weight, however, so the stick flipped back and forth like a seventh leg on an ant.

Brian scratched his head. He could remember few times, if any, that Jamie had imitated something he had done. He was flattered. Impulsively, he reached out and patted Jamie on the back.

It was nearly a half hour later that the little party of men and boys, tired now and walking with less spring in their steps, arrived at the lake. They surveyed it carefully.

The lake was not big and it was not designed for recreation. It was a wilderness lake; there were no boats and no fishermen. Perhaps two hundred yards long by fifty yards wide, it had appeared all at once through the trees. The water was more green than blue and conspicuously full of organic matter. There was no beach at all; the trees ended and the water began. Around the perimeter a thin ring of black mud just a few feet wide marked the boundary between solid earth and the gently rippling waves. For all that, the lake possessed a wild, unspoiled beauty that made Brian wonder if it might be wrong to violate the privacy of this pristine body of water.

Two or three of the boys let out whoops of delight and broke into a run when they saw the water. Jason reached the shore first, stepped onto the mud, and promptly sank up to his knees. When Chad Livingston saw that, he broke into a run, too, and began shouting instructions for the boys to stay back.

He was too late. By the time he reached the shore, four of the scouts were already in the mud, sloshing and sliding around like barnyard hogs. Chad gave orders to retreat from the mud immediately. Reluctantly, the boys obeyed. Back on solid ground, they lined up while the assistant scoutmaster inspected their outfits. The boys' thighs were brown and caked with patches of oily mud. They were wearing shorts, so the dirt was mostly on their bodies. However, their shoes oozed brown streams of water and made a little sucking sound with every step.

There was one thing to be grateful for.

No one had started throwing mud.

Worrying about the uniforms seemed pointless. Even Chad could do nothing to remedy the situation. Since the boys wore swimming trunks underneath, he merely told them to take off the muddy uniforms, and waved his arm in the general direction of the lake. Eagerly they stripped to their swimming suits, rushed to the shore, and—avoiding the mud hole this time—jumped into the water. Two of the other boys peeled off their still-clean uniforms and joined the happy melee. Within seconds the boys were splashing around and flipping water at each other like seals at the zoo.

Except for one. Jamie watched the other boys attentively, but kept his distance from the water. If one of them happened to move a step or two in his direction, he would squeal and run back even farther into the trees. He was not, however, totally immune to the water fun. When the boys began splashing water in each other's faces, he squealed again and started jumping up and down.

Chad turned his attention away form the water fight to watch Jamie. "He get excited like this very often?" he asked Brian.

"Not usually." Brian turned his head to look at his son as he answered the question. Then he moved closer to Jamie. "The boys are in the lake, Jamie," he said. "They're having fun. Do you want to get into your swimming suit and go in the water, too?"

"Fun," echoed Jamie.

"Yes, it is fun," his father repeated. Brian pointed to the lake. "Here, Jamie, I'll help you take off your shirt and pants so you can get in the water. You can play with the other boys."

Jamie eyed the other boys hungrily. For a moment, Brian thought he might go for it. But then Jamie shook his head vigorously and waved his arms. "Okay," he snorted. "Okay!" But he didn't come forward. Instead, he retreated into the woods.

Brian backed away. "Okay, Jamie," he conceded. "You don't have to go in the water. Come back, please."

Jamie stopped. He looked at his father but he stayed put. Brian turned back to Chad. "Well, that's the way it goes," he philosophized. "You can lead a horse to water but you can't make him drink. Can't make Jamie do something he doesn't want to do, either." Brian shrugged his shoulders. Then he walked over to a fallen tree and sat down on the trunk.

Chad had been watching Jamie again. He walked over to where Brian sat on the log. When he was close enough to be easily heard, Chad asked, "How much does Jamie understand when you talk to him?"

There was honest curiosity in the question, but no censure. Brian looked up at Chad as he considered the question. "Well," he answered finally, "Jamie seems to understand simple commands and other basic words pretty well. For example, he knows what you want when you ask him to bring something, like a plate or a banana or something like that. But if you talk about abstract concepts like big and small, or even colors, that's a problem for him. Even at that, he understands so much more than he can say — talking is really hard for him. He works a hundred times harder than you or I just to grasp and retain one word. I've watched him pick up a new word here and there — like a prospector sifting tiny pieces of gold out of a stream — and then lose it again. Sometimes he tries so hard and the words just don't come. That's when I feel bad for him."

Brian sighed audibly. He looked up again, searching the other man's face, then concluded: "But Jamie does understand quite a bit, and he can do some simple tasks like ask for a drink of water or name his favorite toy. We're grateful for that. Some of these kids have no communication skills at all."

Chad didn't say anything, and he didn't move. He stood silently, leaning his stocky frame against a tree and chewing on a long blade of grass. He seemed to be thinking about what he had just heard, perhaps trying to sort it out and decide how he could relate to the autistic boy scout in his troop.

Brian turned his attention back to the boys. Out of the lake now, the scouts were trying to wash out their muddy clothes. Some were laughing, and they jabbed and poked at each other incessantly.

Chad saw them, too. "You guys hungry?" he piped.

"Yeah, man!" shouted Ryan. Abandoning his muddy uniform for the second time, he dashed for his backpack, which had been dumped in a pile with all the other packs under a tree. The other boys were right behind him.

Chad moved to join them. Brian stayed on the log until the others had all retrieved their lunches and found places to sit down and eat. Then he called to Jamie, who had been watching the other boys from back in the trees: "Let's eat, Jamie. Okay? Go get the lunches."

This time Jamie hustled into action. In no time he had his backpack open and began searching the contents for the paper bag that contained his lunch.

Before he could get his hands on his own food, however, Jamie was interrupted by a second request from his father. "Jamie, would you please bring my lunch to me?" Brian pointed to his backpack, the last in what had once been a whole pile. Jamie snorted and shook his head.

"Jamie, bring me my lunch, please," Brian repeated firmly. This time Jamie stood up. He snagged his father's backpack and rushed it to him, carefully holding his own lunch in his other hand. He handed the backpack to his father and sat down on the ground next to the log. In five seconds he had his mouth fastened like a vise around a peanut butter sandwich.

✦✦✦

The sun was well past the median of the sky when Travis discovered the beaver dam in a dry stream bed on the other side of the lake. The dam, about five or six feet in diameter, was made of logs and dirt. While the structure was now high and dry, pools of water above and below testified that a few weeks earlier it had been in the middle of a flowing stream.

Travis pulled one of the logs out of the dam and examined it. "Look at this, guys!" he exclaimed. "Get a load of this log. It's like chewed all over with teeth marks."

The other boys crowded around to see the piece of wood. It was about two feet long and five inches in diameter. Sure enough, both ends were neatly severed by what almost looked like hatchet strokes. But, for all that, it was only a log, and for young boys it lacked the sustaining interest of, say, *Donkey Kong*. Chucking the log, Travis began poking around the dam, looking for beavers, but there was no sign of life. Soon the boys left the beaver mound and began working their way on up the stream bed.

Jamie had observed from a distance the activity at the beaver dam. For whatever reason he still declined to mingle with the other boys. When they left the beaver dam, however, he followed them. He was careful not to stray too far away from his father.

A few yards above the beaver dam the creek bed widened considerably. It was grassy at that point and relatively free of rocks. When Ryan saw the grassy area, he turned and ran back to the lake where the backpacks were stacked under a tree. Moments later he returned with a miniature Nerf football in his hand. He motioned for the other guys to gather around. "This place is perfect," he explained. "Let's play a game. Okay?"

Jeremy's eyes lit up. "All right," he concurred. "Let's go for it!" Soon the boys had made two piles of rocks to mark the goal lines. Then they divided into teams. Ryan chose Kelly and Jason to be on his team. Jeremy, who took command of the other team, selected Travis and Michael to play on his side.

Jeremy's team kicked the ball first. Jason picked it up from the turf and ran for the goal line. Travis chased him and tagged him on the back with both hands to stop the play. After that, the boys lined up with two from each team on the line of scrimmage and one in the backfield. Kelly hiked the ball between his legs to

Ryan. Ryan ran to his left and picked up a few yards before he was tagged by Michael, still well short of the goal line.

Ryan's team stepped back into a huddle. Moments later they were at the line again. This time Ryan took the snap, held the ball for a moment, and threw it to Jason, who was speeding down the side of the stream bed. Unfortunately, the missile was way off target and landed in the trees at the side of the wash. Jason scooped it up and carried it back to the line of scrimmage. After two more plays failed to produce a touchdown, Jeremy's team took possession of the ball.

On the sideline, the scoutmaster observed the game with keen interest. He thought seriously about joining the boys on the field, but feared that his superior weight and height would distort what appeared to be an evenly matched contest. So he stayed back and contented himself with watching the action on the field.

An increasingly excited Jamie watched the game with his father. Every time the ball was snapped he chuckled and clapped his hands. After a few minutes he began to bounce up and down with each play. And when Michael outran the players on the other team and scored a touchdown, Jamie jumped up and down and screamed just like the boys on the field.

Jamie's antics after the touchdown did not go unnoticed. Brian saw Kelly tap Ryan on the shoulder, and both boys looked at Jamie. Then Kelly grabbed the football and walked over to where Jamie was standing. "Jamie," he said, watching the other boy carefully to see how he would respond, "do you want to play football with us?" He held up the football and pointed to the other boys on the field. Jamie stepped back. But he eyed the football like a small child gawking hungrily at an ice cream cone.

"Come on, Jamie," Kelly pleaded. "It's lots of fun. Come and play." He started to walk back toward the other boys, motioning with his finger for Jamie to follow.

No one was more surprised than Brian at what happened next. He stared in disbelief as Jamie followed Kelly onto the makeshift football field. Jamie walked slowly, and once or twice he balked as a foot refused to complete the next step. But eventually he made it.

Jamie was standing on the football field with the other scouts.

Kelly said something to the others. Then they lined up in the middle of the field. Travis was over the ball, with Kelly and Michael behind him. Kelly motioned for Jamie to come over and stand by him. Travis hiked the ball to Kelly. Kelly turned and handed it to Jamie. Then he pointed to the goal line. "Run, Jamie," he said. "Run for the goal line. You can do it."

Jamie looked at the ball in his arms. Then he looked at the other boys. He didn't move. He seemed paralyzed.

Kelly put a hand on Jamie's shoulder. Once more he pointed down the field. "Run over there, Jamie," he urged again. He gave Jamie a little push on the back.

Jamie ran.

It would not be accurate to say that he took off like a bullet. It was more like a wobbly arrow. Stiffly and awkwardly he ran, and once or twice he teetered as if he might fall. But he seemed to know where he was going. The other boys ran after him, but not too fast—they made sure he stayed out in front. Moments later he crossed the imaginary goal line, still holding the football. Then the other boys ran to him and slapped him on the back. "Way to go, Jamie!" exclaimed Michael. "That was a great run. You scored a touchdown!" Jamie stood there as still as a tree, clutching the football, his boyish face aglow with wonder and astonishment.

Off to the side, the leader of the boys and the father of the boy was stunned. In a high school football game, the play would have drawn laughs and catcalls. But to Brian, who had seen and played a lot of football, it was the most beautiful play he had ever seen. It was the most *meaningful* play he had ever seen. He could not have been more affected if his son had just scored the winning touchdown in the state championship game.

And when he saw the other boys slapping Jamie on the back, the always-in-control scoutmaster felt himself choking up. He turned away so the boys wouldn't see his face.

Jamie's run marked the end of the football game. Perhaps the other boys sensed that a climactic event had just occurred, or maybe they were just getting tired. In any case, they broke out of the football formation and began walking back toward the lake. Jamie, his face once more stoic and featureless, followed the others. Brian came last.

When they got back to the lake, they found Chad sitting by a stack of sticks and logs of varying sizes. While the others were gone, he had been searching for wood. The boys looked puzzled, so Chad explained what the poles were for: "I got some sticks so we could practice doing knots and lashings. We're going to build a little tower with these poles." He motioned for the boys to join him. Slowly they gathered around and sat down by him.

But Jamie wasn't interested in tying knots. Apparently, he decided that he had been at the lake long enough, so he pulled on his father's arm. "Go," he said. He picked up his backpack and put it on his shoulders. Then he moved away and began pacing restlessly back and forth between two trees.

Brian turned to the others. "Jamie seems to think it's time to go back. What do the rest of you think?"

Most of the boys seemed to agree—at least about not doing the knots. They looked tired. Brian looked at Chad. "Maybe we better skip the knots for today," he suggested.

Chad grimaced. He glared at Brian. "Don't you think we should do something to work on skills before we go back?" he asked pointedly. He took off his orange cap and brushed off a couple of specs of dirt with his finger.

Brian wasn't sure what to do. He looked at each of the boys again, studying their faces. Then he glanced at his watch; the afternoon was nearly gone. Turning to Chad, he said simply, "I think we better go." The assistant scoutmaster gazed at Brian again, then nodded. Turning, Chad instructed the boys to begin packing up their stuff.

Even then the boys were slow to respond. The long hike, followed by the excitement at the lake and the football game, had consumed much of their otherwise boundless energy. Their initial response to the command to pack up was a big zero. Chad had to walk around and pull several of them to their feet to get them going.

Meanwhile, Jamie was already moving. As soon as the others were on their feet, he took off backtracking through the forest.

"Wait, Jamie," Brian shouted. "We're coming. Just wait a minute, okay?"

Jamie stopped but he didn't return to the group. Muttering to himself, he paced around in the trees while the others picked up their backpacks and prepared to leave. As soon as they started moving, he took off again, staying ten or fifteen yards in front. No one tried to catch up; the boys and their leaders seemed content just to plod along behind.

Jamie marched ahead determinedly, never pausing or looking back for guidance. Chad touched Brian on the arm. Pointing to Jamie, he asked, "How does he know where he's going? There's no trail here at all. Just trees and turf in every direction. I'm not sure some of the rest of us, including me, could find our way back so easily."

Brian shrugged. "He just has a good memory for things like this," he explained. "I guess you might say it's a talent of his. He always seems to know where he is and where he's been."

A few minutes later the hikers reached the edge of the rise and began the descent. Brian was grateful to be going downhill. He was feeling very tired, and the aching in his legs and back suggested that he would likely have sore muscles tomorrow. As he plodded along, arching his body backward to compensate for the steep slope, he reflected on the day's events. They hadn't made a tower. But no one had drowned. No bones had been broken. The scouts seemed to be having a good time. All things considered, the activity at the lake had turned out okay.

The shadows of the trees were long and deep when the boy scouts and their leaders finally arrived at the bottom of the hill. The boys let out a whoop when they saw the van. Everyone crowded around that precious link with civilization. As he removed his backpack and helped Jamie shed his own gear, Brian surveyed his boys. They didn't make a pretty picture with their sweaty faces and mud-streaked clothes. But Brian knew their mothers would accept them no matter how they looked. He gazed at his own son and wondered for the thousandth time what was going on inside that mysterious mind. How did *Jamie* feel about today's experience? It was hard to tell. The kid had experienced his share of ups and downs, for sure.

Then Brian remembered the look on Jamie's face when he scored the touchdown. He smiled. Jamie's mind might be a mystery, but — on that occasion, at least — his face had been as easy to read as the names in a phone book. Somehow, remembering that face made the whole day seem worthwhile.

One by one, the boys of Troop 328 climbed into the van, sank wearily into their seats and fastened their seat belts. Most of them were laughing and joking and poking as they settled down for the ride home. The scoutmaster took a final look around the van to make sure that everyone was in place. Then he started the engine and eased the van onto the road back to Colorado Springs.

Chapter Eleven
July 1994

Summer was at its peak in the Colorado Rockies. After a wet spring, the mountains were unusually green for the middle of the summer. Some of the high peaks still displayed patches of snow. The insect count was also unusually high. At least, that's the way it appeared from the number of tiny smashed carcasses on the windshield. Nature flourished all around the brown Suburban as it sped down the winding mountain road. With Chad Livingston at the wheel, the car flew up and down like a roller coaster. The other occupants of the car seemed to be enjoying the bouncy ride.

Troop 328 was returning home after five days at Alexander Scout Camp.

Brian leaned back in his seat and closed his eyes. This was the longest camping trip of the summer for his scout troop. It had been a good week; the boys had learned a lot and had a lot of fun. High adventure was great, but right now he was looking forward to some rest and relaxation. By this time tomorrow he'd be finding his adventure in a good book. He smiled and leaned back further in his seat.

But tomorrow wasn't here yet, and Brian's mind got pulled back quickly to the present by Chad's voice. "Hey, Spencer," the assistant scoutmaster called out from his position behind the wheel, "What time are they expecting us to pull in today?"

"We said we'd be back about 4:00," Brian responded as he sat up and opened his eyes. "Why?"

Chad was checking his watch. "Let's see. It's just a little past noon. And we have about an hour and a half of driving to get back to Colorado Springs. So we're ahead of schedule, right?"

"Yeah, I guess we are. And that's fine with me. I'm ready to get back."

Chad didn't seem to be listening. "Since we have some extra time," he said, "How about making a little stop at Knobby Cave?"

"Where?"

"Knobby Cave."

"Never heard of it."

"It's on the trail to Crystal Lake. About a half mile off the road. We could take the boys up there and be back in less than two hours. Still get home in time."

The prospect of yet another hike—especially one that led to a cave—was not particularly appealing to Brian. "What's in Knobby Cave?" he asked, more out of suspicion than curiosity.

"Well, it's a very interesting place," replied the assistant scoutmaster. "Limestone cave, with lots of different rock formations. There's a lot of little round globules that were formed by dripping water. They look like little knobs of putty. That's where the cave gets its name. My cousin took me there once a few years ago. I've been wanting to go back."

"Is this cave . . . safe?"

"Sure. I guess not too many people know about it. But some, like my cousin Rex, have been there many times. There's no shafts or pits or anything like that in the cave. When I went there, we just climbed in, walked down the main tunnel to the cavern where the knobs are, and then came back out. No sweat."

Brian was doubtful. He didn't like caves. He considered himself an intelligent person who was beyond irrational fears;

however, if there was a chink anywhere in the armor of his self-confidence, it was a tendency to feel uneasy in close, tight places. Caves were tight places. Dark, cold, tight places. Exploring caves appealed to him about as much as receiving unexpected mail from the IRS. Not that he couldn't handle it. He just didn't enjoy it. "You sure this is a good idea?" he asked again.

"Really, Brian, I'm telling you it's no big deal. What say we ask the boys and see if they want to stop? If they do, we could at least walk up to the cave. It's not that far from the road. Then, if we don't want to go in, we just come back to the car and drive on home. We've been traveling for over an hour now. The boys would probably like to get out of the car."

Brian sighed and nodded reluctantly. "Okay," he said. "See what the boys say about it." He secretly hoped that the scouts, who were also tired and anxious to get home, would pour cold water on the whole idea and squelch it.

Chad lost no time in following up. "Hey, guys," he yelled in a voice that carried all the way to the back seat. "You want to stop at Knobby Cave?"

The boys became silent; nobody answered the question. Chad repeated it. "Who wants to stop at Knobby Cave?"

This time they heard the last word, at least. "What cave?" asked Ryan.

"Knobby Cave," was the patient reply. "It's just a few miles ahead, a little bit off the road."

"What's there?" the boy asked, a hint of suspicion in his voice. Maybe he suspected some kind of work activity or passing off the requirements for another merit badge. Or maybe he was just tired, like his scoutmaster.

Chad pressed forward. He repeated the explanation he had given earlier to Brian. Then he asked each boy individually if he wanted to see the cave. The boys seemed ready for a break, with or without spelunking, so Chad had little difficulty mustering support for the cave activity.

There was one other matter to take care of. "We need flashlights," Chad said as he turned to Brian again. "How many do we have?"

"I think just about every boy has a flashlight," replied the scoutmaster, trying to stir up a little self-enthusiasm. "And we have our electric lantern. We should have enough." He turned around to the boys and asked, "How many of you guys have got flashlights?" All hands but one went up.

"Where's your flashlight, Jason?"

The boy shrugged his shoulders. "I forgot to bring one. But I didn't really need it, anyways."

"That's okay," said Brian. He stopped to count on his fingers. "That's five flashlights, counting mine, plus the lantern. Should be enough, don't you think?"

"Sure," said the other man. "We'll only be in there about an hour, if that."

"Okay, looks like we're set." Brian tried to sound excited. In his mind he determined to just sit back and let Chad run the show. He didn't know anything about where they were going, anyway. He would bring up the rear and make sure no one got separated from the group on the hike or in the cave. A couple of hours and they'd be on the road again.

Ten minutes later Chad pulled off the road into a small parking area. A weather-beaten sign announced the beginning of the trail to Crystal Lake. Brian saw a narrow path leading off into the trees. It was a second-class trail, unpaved and not very wide.

Before starting the hike, they gathered around the car and ate a quick lunch of sandwiches and brownies. The soft drinks and punch that they brought to camp had long since disappeared, so they had to drink water. Some of the boys were not used to drinking water. They grumbled but drank it anyway. After they had eaten, Chad told the boys to fill up their canteens from the big water container in the back of the car. Then he had them check their flashlights to make sure they were working.

After that, he instructed the boys to bring their canteens and flashlights with them, and they started up the trail.

Chad led the way. The boys followed him in single file. Brian came last. There were five boys, including Jamie who marched along the trail just in front of his father. The trail climbed up a narrow canyon, gradually at first, then more steeply. A cool breeze wafted down the canyon, and the path was mostly shaded by tall pine trees, so the hikers felt relatively comfortable. A little brook gurgled softly in the background as it trickled down the canyon; the hikers crossed it two or three times—jumping from rock to rock to keep their feet from getting wet—as they wound their way up the trail. The chatter of birds was incessant, and once they saw a squirrel run across the path in front of them. Even Brian was feeling better now about this little excursion.

After they had climbed for about half an hour, Chad stopped and motioned for the others to gather around him. At that point the trail ran flush against the right side of the canyon wall. Above them the rocky face angled sharply upward for sixty or seventy feet, gradually melting into the background of the deep blue sky.

Chad pointed to a spot part way up the side of the cliff.

"There it is," he crowed. "There's the entrance to Knobby Cave."

The boys strained to follow the pointing finger. Some of them gasped when they saw the tiny opening in the cliff face. It was not what they had expected, and it was very exciting.

"Awesome," said Jason.

Brian stared at the little black hole in disbelief. Perhaps three feet high by two feet wide, it was at least fifty feet above the trail and seemed to be etched right into the side of the mountain. It didn't open directly into the cliff wall, but rather into an overhang that jutted out perpendicular to the cliff. Looking back down the direction they had come, Brian could see the overhang and the opening above him.

"This is crazy," he muttered to himself. He had expected to find some kind of tunnel at the side of the trail. "How would we ever get up there?" He turned to face the assistant scoutmaster. "You must be joking about this whole thing, Chad. No way are we going to climb up the side of that cliff with these boys."

Chad grinned, apparently savoring every minute of the stir he had created. "Hold on, Brian," he drawled. "It's not near as bad as it looks. There's a ledge up there. See it? It goes right along the face of the cliff from the rock slide to the cave entrance. Probably where some of the runoff that goes into the cave comes from. All we have to do is climb up the rock slide. Then we can walk over to the cave and go inside. It's almost like a trail."

Brian followed Chad's pointing finger. Twenty-five or thirty yards ahead of them a rock slide tumbled down the side of the canyon across the trail and into the stream bed below. The canyon wall was less steep there, and he could see that the rock slide could be climbed with a little effort. Stepping back from the face of the cliff, he looked up above him to see if he could discover the ledge that led to the cave. He spotted it, a thin line that went all the way from the rock slide over to the mouth of the cave.

"How wide is the ledge?" he asked.

"Plenty wide," Chad replied. "I'd say it's about three feet wide, at least. Just like a trail. You walk up the rocks, then go straight across to the cave. And, bingo, you're inside."

Brian wasn't sure it would be that easy. A naturally cautious man, he tried to work through the pros and cons of taking the boys up to the cave. The ledge bothered him. He had imagined that they would hike up to the cave, poke their heads inside, and head back down the trail. But it was clearly more complicated than that, and he didn't like it. He was about to suggest skipping the cave exploration and turning back. Before he could say anything, however, Chad ran down the trail, scampered up the rock slide, and positioned himself above the other hikers on the ledge. "Come on, guys," he yelled. "Let's go!"

Most of the boys followed immediately. Within a few seconds, only Brian, Jamie, and Greg remained on the trail. The two boys looked at Brian uncertainly. Shrugging his shoulders, he took Jamie by the hand and motioned for Greg to follow them over to the rock slide. Jamie seemed willing to accompany him. That was encouraging. The last thing he wanted right now was a struggle trying to get Jamie to do something that neither of them wanted to do.

He picked his way up the rock slide, still holding Jamie's hand. Negotiating the rocks was a bit tricky. The rock slide was steep, and some of the rocks were small, so there was some danger of dislodging a stone and slipping down. However, they climbed slowly and reached the top without mishap. Chad had come back to meet them. He gave Brian a hand and helped Brian and Jamie off the rocks onto the ledge. Brian eyed the ledge critically. It *was* wide enough, he decided. Two to three feet wide — four in some places. Cautiously, he loosened his grip on Jamie's hand. "This way, Jamie," he said softly. As he started moving, he looked back over his shoulder and discovered that Jamie was following him. The boy walked nonchalantly along the ledge, seemingly unconcerned about the cliff to his right. That made Brian a little nervous, but soon they reached the end of the ledge where the others were waiting.

At the entrance to the cave, Chad motioned for the boys to flatten back against the side of the cliff and look at him. Pointing to the dark hole, he said: "All right, you guys, listen up. We're going inside. It's kind of tight at the beginning, but it opens up big after a few feet. I want you to stay together. I'll be in front, Mr. Spencer will be at the back. Everyone stays together. Okay? First time somebody starts goofing off, we come right back out. Now, let's go."

Chad glanced at the boys to make sure they were ready. Then he picked up the electric lantern, which he had carried up from the car, and turned on the powerful beam. Holding the lantern in front of him, he got down on his knees and crawled into the cave. Cautiously, and almost in slow motion, the boys followed him.

Soon everyone had entered the cave but Jamie and his father. Jamie poked his head into the opening. Apparently he didn't like what he saw, for a moment later he came right back out, stood up, and leaned back against the cliff wall. Brian turned on his flashlight and carefully moved up beside his son. "Come on, Jamie," he coaxed, "Let's go inside. It's all right. See, I have a light here." He spoke very softly, trying to sound calm and confident. But when he looked into Jamie's face, he saw fear, perhaps even panic, in the boy's eyes.

Suddenly the situation had turned serious. Brian didn't like trying to maneuver around on the ledge with a reluctant and unpredictable boy at his side. Slowly he turned around and squatted down with his back to the hole in the rock. He took hold of Jamie's hand. Jamie hadn't moved in some time. He pressed back against the cliff, obviously terrified of the cave.

"Come with me, Jamie," Brian urged again. Brian was beginning to feel afraid, too. He had no idea what Jamie would do next. He had to get Jamie out of this situation, away from the cliff. He pulled more firmly on the boy's arm. Jamie grew tense and tried to pull his hand away. "No," he cried. "No go!"

Brian heard the terror in his son's voice and knew he had to act quickly. The cave seemed the safest place. Taking a firm grip on Jamie's arm, he leaned backward and pulled the boy inside the cave on top of him. Jamie started to wiggle and squirm, but Brian put his arms around him and held him tight. Brian was grateful for his extra size and strength. "It's okay, Jamie," he whispered, trying to stay calm. "I'm here with you. You're okay."

For what seemed like an hour but was probably just a minute or two, Brian held on while Jamie screamed and twisted and fought to get free. Finally he stopped struggling. Brian held him tight for a minute or two longer. Then, still gripping the flashlight with his arm clasped around Jamie's back, he began inching his way backward into the cave. Soon he felt hands grasping him and Jamie, pulling them back a little further, then lifting them to their feet.

Once through the narrow opening, the cave was large enough to stand up in. The glow from Chad's lantern lit up the cave and cast eerie shadows on the walls. As soon as he and Jamie were inside, Brian moved in front of the entrance to block any attempt by his son to escape. Then he stopped to catch his breath.

"Sorry," Brian said to the others. "I guess Jamie didn't want to come in here."

No one said a word. Jamie was still breathing hard, but his body was still. The other boys acted like they didn't know what to do or say. Finally Chad broke the silence. "I'm sorry, too," he said. "We should have given you some help. I just didn't think about it. Sorry." He turned away and began inspecting the cave.

Help me how? Brian thought angrily. A lot of good it would have done to have Chad and all these boys out there thrashing around on that ledge. He bit his lip, however, and said nothing to the others.

When Jamie and Brian had recovered, Chad stepped forward, and, motioning for the others to follow him, began moving into the passageway. One by one, the boys fell in place behind him. Brian motioned for Jamie to follow the other boys. Jamie obeyed, but Brian detected a small whimpering sound as they began to move deeper into the cave. Brian went with misgivings of his own, anxious to get in and get out.

They had entered a strange world. The passageway they traversed was four or five feet wide and seven or eight feet high. It was cool inside the cave—much cooler than outside in the midday July sun. Everything looked black except for the intermittent flashlight beams that danced around the floor and walls of the passageway like flood lights probing the nighttime sky.

The most noticeable thing in the cave was the sound, or, more accurately, the lack of sound. There were no more bird calls. No murmuring brook. No wind whistling through the trees. It was icy quiet. Only the sound of muffled footsteps, punctuated occasionally by scraping noises as some one's boot slid on the rocky floor, penetrated the blanketing silence.

Once or twice as they moved along, the sweeping arc of Brian's flashlight passed over branching tunnels. These were smaller than the main passage, but they were deep enough that the flashlight failed to reveal their endings.

Brian had not expected anything this extensive, and he wondered how big the cave was. He thought about the mountain above them — tons of rock and ore. For a moment he imagined that the rock was closing in around him, trapping him deep inside the mountain. He shook his head and tried to clear his mind. Gradually the sensation passed, but he was more anxious than ever to get to wherever they were going, take a quick look-see, and get back to the outside world.

After they had been walking for perhaps twenty minutes, Brian heard excited conversation ahead. Suddenly the tunnel opened up into a large cavern. The ceiling was high, though still within range of Brian's probing flashlight. As he looked up he could see stalactites hanging down like huge icicles. He judged the circumference of the chamber to be 30 or 40 feet. On the other side of the cavern was a dark opening, apparently the continuation of the tunnel they had been following.

Chad had gathered the boys around him. Borrowing one of the closest flashlights, he illuminated the nearest wall with a triumphant flourish. "There they are, guys," he said. "See all those little globs poking out? Looks like a thousand golf balls — or door knobs — plastered onto the wall. That's why it's called Knobby Cave."

Jason wanted to know what the knobs were made of.

"Limestone," said Chad. "They're made out of stuff that's inside the water. As the water runs down the wall, it leaves a little mineral deposit behind. Give yourself some time, say ten thousand years, and you've got a little ball made out of limestone. If you look closer, you can see that some of the wall is wet even as we speak. That water's been trickling down there for thousands of years, and that's why we have the little globules."

Some of the boys were fingering the walls of the cavern. Brian reached out himself, feeling the cold, smooth stone covered with a perpetual dampness. He wondered what it would be like to be a cold wet rock trapped for eons in this dark hole. He shivered and withdrew his hand.

Jamie's attention span for Chad's geology lesson was brief. Nor did he reach out to touch the walls. After a quick look around, he moved close to his father and took hold of his arm. "Go," he said, pulling on his father's arm.

Some of the others were tiring as well. "What else is there to see in this place?" asked Travis.

"There's an underground lake close by," the assistant scoutmaster responded eagerly. "Would you like to see that?"

"Is it very big?" Travis sounded like he wasn't really sure he wanted to know the answer to the question.

"Well, I haven't actually seen it," admitted Chad. "But I don't think it's too big. More like a pond than a lake, I guess. My cousin told me about it when we were here. He said it's very beautiful. Dark, black water that's cold and still as midnight. Want to see it?"

"Where is it?" Travis looked around curiously.

"You have to go a little farther down the tunnel." Chad pointed his flashlight at the spot where the cavern narrowed again into a smaller passageway. "It's not very far. Five minutes, maybe." He turned to look at Brian. "What do you think, Chief? Should we go on to the lake?"

Brian felt Jamie's little tug on his arm. "Well," he said uncertainly. "We've been in here at least half an hour. Don't you think we should start heading back soon?"

"Yeah, I do. But I really don't think it's very far to the lake. How about we just go on to that point, take a quick look, and then head back to the car?"

"Okay. Let's just do it," Brian consented, happy to have a plan outlined for getting back on their way. He turned to Jamie. "Jamie, we're going to go just a little farther into the cave," he whispered in the boy's ear. "We're almost there. Then we'll go back to the car."

"Go home," said Jamie. He pulled again on his father's arm, tugging him back in the direction they had come.

"I'm sorry, Jamie. I know you don't like it in here," Brian said, still speaking quietly in Jamie's ear. "I don't really like it that well, either. But we need to go just a little bit farther. Come on, son."

He took Jamie by the hand and followed the others into the tunnel.

Once again they walked in silence, Chad leading the way and Brian bringing up the rear. The passageway opened up before them, taking them deeper and deeper into the cave. It was difficult to measure the passage of time in the dark, monotonous cave. However, they had clearly been walking for much longer than five minutes when Chad called a halt. "I'm not sure we're going in the right direction," he confessed. "We should have been there by now. I think maybe we should just give up on the lake and head back." There was a trace of disappointment in his voice, but even his excitement for exploration had diminished as the little troop moved further into unfamiliar territory.

"Aren't we almost there?" asked Ryan. He, too, sounded a little disappointed at not finding the lake.

"Well, I thought we would be there by now, for sure," replied the assistant scoutmaster. "But . . . well, Ryan, like I said earlier, I haven't really seen the lake myself. I don't know how close we are. But I think we'd better go back. What do you say, Skipper?"

"Let's go back," said the scoutmaster.

So they turned around and began walking back the way they had come. Brian stepped aside while Chad moved out in front again. Then he squeezed Jamie's hand and nudged him forward. "Let's go, Jamie," he whispered. "I don't know about you but I'll be glad to get back to the sunlight and the trees. I think it was worth coming in here, though." He knew Jamie probably didn't understand what he was saying, but he didn't mind. He felt a need to talk. And if the boy didn't understand everything, at least he didn't disagree.

Once again they tramped single file through the tunnel. Brian was thinking about how tired he felt. He just wanted to get back on the road, back to Colorado Springs, back to his home where he could relax. Being in charge of these boys for a week had taken a lot out of him. He thought about the boys, visualizing them one at a time in his mind's eye. Each one was different. There was Ryan, the rowdy one. Rough and tough. Always had to be the top guy. Then there was Greg, the new one this year. Greg was just the opposite of Ryan: not too outgoing; definitely not an athlete; a good student, though. No wonder this job was a challenge, trying to meet the needs of those two boys at the same time. Not to mention the others.

Not to mention Jamie. He thought about that one for awhile, too. Jamie was a boy scout. And he was Jamie's scoutmaster. He was . . .

Brian almost bumped into the object of his ruminations. Jamie had stopped suddenly. Brian caught himself and regained his balance. He discovered that all of the boys had stopped. The next thing he knew Chad was beside him, speaking quietly so the others couldn't hear. "Brian," he whispered earnestly, "we should be there by now. We should be back to the cavern."

At first Brian didn't comprehend what Chad was saying. "What are you talking about, Chad? What do you mean, we should be back to the cavern by now? We're not there yet, but we must be close. We've been walking out almost as long as we walked in."

"That's what I mean," said the other man. "Brian, I'm not sure exactly how long we've been going—it's so hard to keep track of time down here—but I think we should be back to the large room by now. I've been thinking for the last few minutes we should be there. I'm wondering if we got in the wrong tunnel somewhere."

"The wrong tunnel!" Unconsciously, Brian raised his voice. Chad motioned with his hand to speak softer, so Brian lowered the volume, if not the intensity, of his voice. "What are you talking about, Chad? There's only one tunnel and we're in it."

Chad shook his head. "There's more than one tunnel. I noticed some shafts branching off in two or three places when we were going in. It bothered me a little at the time, but I didn't really worry too much about it because I thought I had kept track of things pretty well. Now I'm not so sure."

"So you don't know if we're in the tunnel that goes back to the large cavern?"

"Right." The uncertainty in Chad's voice was evident, now. "I thought we were in the right one. But, Brian, I'm pretty sure we should be there by now. We may be getting farther and farther away from where we need to be."

These words struck the scoutmaster with a chill that penetrated much deeper than the damp, cool air of the cave. "Chad, are you trying to say we're lost? You can't be serious. We haven't gone anywhere to be lost. Look, the chamber with all the knobby rocks is probably just ahead. Let's go on a little farther and see if we find it. Just don't panic, okay?"

"So who's panicking? I'm just saying that I think we should back up a ways and see if we can find the right branch of the tunnel. I really don't think we're in the right tunnel, Brian."

The two scoutmasters stood there silently for a minute or two, neither of them moving or talking, afraid of alarming the boys, but uncertain about how to proceed. Suddenly Brian thought about the implications of being lost in a cave with a group of young boys, and fear flared up in his mind. He pushed it back, trying to talk calmly to himself. He tried to think. What should they do? If they continued on, they risked getting deeper and deeper into some uncharted branch of this abominable cave. But if they turned back, and the cavern was just ahead . . .

"Let's go on a little farther," he said hoarsely. "If we don't get to the cavern in five minutes, we'll double back." Chad nodded. The assistant scoutmaster took a deep breath and let it out slowly. Then he walked back up to the front of the line.

"We were just trying to figure out how much farther it is to the big room with all the knobs," he explained to the boys. Then he started walking again. One by one, the boys fell in line. If they sensed that something was wrong, they didn't say anything about it.

As they tramped through the tunnel, Brian looked around with considerably more attention than he had shown before. He watched for any new tunnels branching off, but saw none. He pointed his flashlight at the floor of the cave, seeking evidence of their previous passage in the opposite direction, but the ground was so hard and rocky that no footprints were visible in either direction. He tried to fix in his mind the shape and size of the tunnel they were in. It looked so much like the other parts of the cave they had been in before. Maybe the ceiling was lower here, the walls a bit closer, but it was hard to be sure.

After a few minutes they stopped again. They had not reached the large circular chamber. Brian and Chad consulted briefly. Then they spoke to the boys.

It was Chad who did the talking. "Uh, we have a little problem, guys," he said, choosing his words carefully. "We think we might have turned off into the wrong tunnel back there a little ways. Did any of you notice turning the wrong way?"

No one answered.

"Do you see anything that would tell you if we're in the right tunnel?" asked Brian. "I mean, did you notice anything on the way down to the lake that could tell us whether we're in the same tunnel now as we were then? A mark on the wall of the cave, maybe, or a certain piece of rock?"

Again, no one spoke. Apparently, none of the boys knew where they were either.

"Well, we're going to backtrack just a little ways and see if there's another branch of the cave that we missed," said Chad. "All of you follow me, and look closely to see if you recognize anything. Oh, and just as a precaution, let's save our flashlights, okay? All of you turn your lights off. I'll keep my lantern on to guide us."

"Are we lost, Mr. Livingston?" The question came from Travis, the patrol leader.

"Well, not exactly. I wouldn't say we're lost," replied the assistant scoutmaster. "We just made a wrong turn back there. We'll go back and find the right tunnel and then we'll be on our way."

"Then why are you having us turn off our flashlights?"

"Just a safety procedure, Travis. We just want to save our resources as much as possible. But, don't worry. Everything's going to be all right."

And, with that, he turned and started back down the tunnel. Back the way they had come. The others followed. All but Jamie. He stood in the middle of the tunnel, looking in the opposite direction. Brian pointed after the others and nudged Jamie to follow them.

"This one," said Jamie, pointing in the direction they had been going before.

"No, Jamie. We have to go back the other way. I know you want to get out of here, and so do I. But we need to go back and find the right way. Come on." He took hold of the boy's hand and started after the others.

Jamie winced and tried to get away. "Owie," he cried.

But his father was in no mood to argue. Not wanting to lose contact with the others, he hustled after them, dragging Jamie behind him. After several yards of scraping his feet the other way, Jamie gave up and fell in step with his father.

Soon they caught up with the others and joined their silent trek through the dark limestone passage.

◆◆◆

Brian slumped wearily to his knees. He sat down on the lumpy floor of the cave and braced his back against the cold, unyielding stone wall. Part of his brain was strangely numb while another part raced madly. He tried once more to piece together what had happened to him and his troop of boy scouts.

They were trapped inside a cave.

He still couldn't believe they were lost. He shook his head to see if he could force himself awake from this nightmare.

But it wasn't a dream. He couldn't see much of his surroundings, but he could feel them. The cold rock. The penetrating dampness of this cursed pit.

According to his watch, it was 9:18 p.m. That meant they had been inside the cave for eight or nine hours. Most of that time they had been searching for a way out, casually at first and then with greater and greater urgency. Their situation was not yet desperate, but things had gone much too far to be taken casually now.

Back and forth through the tunnels they had tramped. But they had not found the large cavern again, much less an opening to the outside world. Brian shook his head again. He had the impression that the cave was not large. Perhaps they had been going around in circles, or back and forth along the same tunnel. Maybe it was just bad luck. Whatever the case, they had not found the right branch—the one that would take them back to the surface. Back to the warm air. Back to the trees. Back to the sun. Back to the car that would take them home.

It occurred to Brian that it would be dark outside by now. He didn't care. The moon would be as beautiful as the sun. Any kind of light would be welcome.

Right now the cave was cloaked in darkness. When he and his companions, exhausted, had finally stopped to rest before making another try at escaping from the cave, they had extinguished all of the lights to conserve energy

All at once the darkness got to him. Brian felt a wave of panic building inside his body. He took a deep breath and tried to suppress the fear. For just a moment he felt smothered by the rock around him. He wanted to get up and run screaming down the corridor. He took another deep breath and closed his eyes. Gradually the feeling of desperation passed.

They had to find the way out of this place. They had a little water—whatever the boys had brought in their canteens when they set out on the hike—but no food. The most immediate concern was light. Without light their chances of getting out would be considerably less. Trying to conserve their battery power, they had used only one flashlight at a time. Two flashlights were already spent; the others could not be expected to last much longer. Even the big electric lantern would not last indefinitely.

Brian put out his hand to find Jamie. He recalled sadly how frustrated and troubled the boy had seemed as Brian had been forced on several occasions to drag him unwillingly through tunnels. Now Jamie sat motionless and silent at his side. He doesn't understand what's going on, Brian thought. For once he was grateful for Jamie's limitations.

One of the other boys was crying. Brian couldn't tell who it was in the dark. Jason, maybe. He wished he could somehow reach out and comfort the boy. He wished he could comfort all of them—every boy who had wept or cried out or begged for help that afternoon. But there wasn't much he could do. Assurances that they would soon be out of the cave just didn't do the job anymore.

He winced as he pondered their plight. What a stupid thing to do, coming in here. He lashed himself mentally for ever consenting to do it against his better judgment. They must find a way out! And they had to do it themselves. Rescue from the outside was unlikely. Of course someone would come looking for them. They would find the car, and begin scouring the countryside for the missing scout troop. They might search for days without ever thinking about the cave. Again he chided himself for coming in such a place without telling anyone where they were going.

Brian said a silent but fervent prayer: "Dear God. Please help us get out of this terrible place! For the boys' sake. Please."

He leaned back against the cold stone wall. A heavy weariness took possession of his body. He was so tired. So tired, and so afraid.

✦✦✦

A pain in his back woke Brian from his fitful dozing. He rubbed his body where the piece of rock had been poking him. Slowly the memory of where he was seeped back into his consciousness. He sat up, trying to penetrate the gloom with his eyes. It was too dark to see anything. He listened and heard sounds of deep and regular breathing. Some of the boys were sleeping. Well, let them sleep. A little rest might be a valuable asset in the hours ahead.

Brian sighed and leaned back against the rock. Almost instinctively he reached out beside him to make sure that Jamie was all right.

His groping hand found nothing but the hard stone of the cave.

Brian was on his knees instantly, crawling further into the darkness. There was nothing there. He turned and crawled in the other direction until he bumped into one of the boys.

It was not Jamie.

He jumped to his feet. "Jamie," he shouted. "Jamie, where are you?" He fumbled for his flashlight, turned it on and swept the beam rapidly around the cave.

Chad jumped up. "What is it, Brian? What's wrong?"

"It's Jamie," he gasped hoarsely. "I can't find him. Help me find him!"

Quickly they checked off the members of the group. Everyone was accounted for — except Jamie. He was not there with the others.

Pushing Chad in one direction, Brian ran the other way. "Stay here," he commanded the boys. "Don't move until we get back. We have to find Jamie. Don't move!"

With the echoes of his command still reverberating through the cave, Brian rushed off into the darkness.

◆◆◆

The little figure crept awkwardly but purposefully through the dark tunnel. He moved instinctively, without light, fingers sliding along the cave wall to guide him through the passage. Three times he came to forks in the tunnel. Each time he paused momentarily, sensing rather than seeing the junction. And each time he followed his instincts and stepped ahead into the darkness.

"Go home," he said softly to himself. "Car."

He was tired of the dark cave, tired of being pulled around in circles. He wanted to be outside. If he could just get back to the car, everything would be all right.

After a time he arrived at the circular chamber with the knobby walls. He felt the tunnel open up on either side. Carefully, he picked his way around the wall of the cavern until he found the opening on the other side. Without hesitation, he plunged into the tunnel and pressed forward. He knew he was getting close.

When he came to the outside entrance, he crouched down and squeezed into the narrow crawl space. He was squealing with excitement as he popped through the opening and felt a breath of warm air on his cheeks.

"Home," he exclaimed as he jumped to his feet. An exhilarating feeling filled his head and his chest. Running now, he raced along the path toward the rock slide. He ran as he had run for the touchdown, pumping his body in ungainly and unsteady movements. He completed three steps on the narrow ledge. The fourth step struck the side of the ledge and slid off. He gasped once as he bounced against the side of the cliff and fell. Dislodged by the blow, a shower of small stones clattered down the side of the canyon and a little dust cloud rose up from the valley floor.

When the dust had settled, the body of a boy lay still on the trail to Crystal Lake.

Chapter Twelve
July 1994

They were resting again when they heard the voice.

It was late afternoon on the second day; they had been in the cave over 30 hours. Water and food were gone. Only a feeble beam from the electric lantern separated them from total darkness. All of them were hungry and thirsty. And afraid. They were resting because they were too tired to keep walking—and walking didn't seem to take them anywhere.

Now they were desperate.

That's why they paid no attention to the voice at first. It seemed to be an auditory mirage, a mocking echo from the cave. No one stirred. Several minutes passed.

"Hullo," cried the voice. "Hullo. Anybody in here?" Though faint and far away, it was clearly a voice. This time all of them heard and understood the words. They stumbled to their feet.

"We're here," yelled Brian. He had the biggest lungs and the loudest voice. He waited a few seconds and shouted the same words again. After the third time, the other voice answered.

"Stay where you are, but keep talking. We'll find you."

And so they took turns shouting their names, familiar places, favorite foods, whatever came into their minds. Every few seconds the other people would answer—it soon became clear that more than one person was in the other party—and each time the voices sounded closer. Within half an hour they were joined by three men. The members of the scout troop shouted and clapped when they saw the lights approaching through the darkness. Some of them cried when they discovered that the newcomers brought water and sandwiches.

"Thank you so much for finding us," Brian whispered huskily as he approached the closest member of the rescue team. "Things were starting to look kind of grim in here."

"You all right?" The man pointed his light at Brian's face to see who he was talking to. "Are you Spencer?" he asked.

"Yeah. I'm Brian Spencer. I'm the scoutmaster. To answer your question, we're tired and hungry, but we're okay — those of us who are here. But one of our scouts — my son — is lost somewhere in these awful tunnels. I'm so glad you're here. Will you help us find him?"

The other man didn't answer right away. He looked questioningly at his companions. Then he faced Brian again. "Mr. Spencer," he said finally, "I'm Terry Dickson, from the County Sheriff's office. We . . . found your son. Outside the cave."

"You found him? Outside the cave? Oh! Is he . . . all right?"

Another pause.

"He fell from the cliff," said the man. He had removed his hat; he fingered it nervously as he spoke. "I'm sorry, Mr. Spencer," he stammered, "but your son is . . . "

The man's mouth moved but no words came out. He took a deep breath, and, with some difficulty, continued. "Your son is dead. We found his body on the trail at the bottom of the cliff. That's how we figured out you were in the cave."

Terry Dickson stopped speaking; he seemed uncertain about what to do. Then he put his hands on Brian's shoulders, and, as well as he could in the dark, looked into his face. "I'm sorry," he said softly. "I wish I didn't have to tell you this. I'd give anything not to have such news at a time like this. If it's any consolation, I think you should know that if it wasn't for your son we wouldn't have found the rest of you. We would never have thought of looking in this cave. None of the original rescue party even knew it was here. We had to send back to Colorado

Springs to find someone who was familiar with the cave so we could come in and look for you." He pointed to another man in the rescue party. "This is Don Thomas. You can thank him, too. He's the one who knows this cave. He brought us in and he will take us back out.

Terry Dickson lifted his hands from Brian's shoulders. "I'm sorry," he repeated as he turned away to talk to the other members of the scout troop. Brian stood petrified, his mind fixed on the devastating message he had just received. After all he had been through in the last two days, it was more than he could handle. Slowly, painfully, he turned away and quietly withdrew from the others. He slumped back against the wall of the cave and slid slowly down to the ground. Putting his head between his hands, he began to cry softly.

"Jamie," he whispered to himself. He thought of the little boy with the freckled face: the boy who didn't understand and couldn't talk; the boy who sat quietly by himself in the corner; the boy who had never quite been his, but who had always owned a big piece of his heart. Jamie was dead. Could such a thing be possible? Surely the boy who had lived and breathed so recently in his memory was still alive. There was no way Jamie could have found his way out of the cave. Maybe the rescue team had found someone else's body. Maybe they thought he was dead but he was only unconscious. Maybe . . .

But when he finally faced himself, Brian knew it was true. Jamie was gone. The boy would no longer be part of his life. It was a bitter pill to swallow, and he choked on it. His head was swimming, his stomach churning. He put his hands behind his neck and pulled his head down toward his knees as he wept in the darkness.

He was still there, pressed against the cold unfeeling rock of the cave, when Chad Livingston came over to him. Unable to speak, Chad waited silently and awkwardly at Brian's side. Then he reached out instinctively, took hold of Brian's hands, and gently helped him to his feet. He put his arms around

Brian's neck and they cried on each other's shoulder. Then Chad put his arm around Brian's waist and helped him over to join the others.

◆◆◆

Marianne leaned into the cello with the full force of her body. Like a long knife attached to her hand, the big mahogany bow cut into the strings, unleashing a melody that saturated the room with beauty and sorrow. For several minutes she poured her whole soul into the *Vocalise*. When she was finished, drops of sweat stood out on her forehead. Her back was killing her, but she ignored it. She sat there for a while, breathing heavily, staring at the big instrument long after the echoes of its music had died.

Only when the doorbell rang did Marianne stir from her position. She carefully put the cello down on the carpet and placed the bow on her music stand. Then she went over to the door and opened it. Candi Jamison was standing on the porch.

"Marianne," she said, reaching out and taking Marianne by the arm. "I've been waiting for an opportunity to come by and talk to you. And I just felt like today was the day."

"Come in, Candi." Marianne stepped back to let the other woman enter and motioned for Candi to sit down on the sofa. Then she sat down beside her.

Neither woman spoke for a moment. Candi searched Marianne's face. She seemed to be searching for the right words as well. She glanced at the cello on the floor. "Looks like you've been playing," she observed.

"Music always helps me when I'm down," answered Marianne.

"Yes, I'm sure it does." Candi looked into Marianne's face again. "You've probably heard this a thousand times in the last few days," she said, "but I just wanted to tell you how sorry I am about what happened."

It was a sincere comment, and Marianne reciprocated. "Thank you, Candi," she replied. "You're very kind. It was nice of you to think of me."

"I came to the funeral, Marianne. It didn't seem like the right time to talk to you so I just stayed in the back and then slipped out. But it was a beautiful service. There was a lovely feeling there."

"It did turn out well," Marianne agreed, "even though it was a difficult time for all of us."

Candi shifted her position on the couch and moved back a little. Once again she seemed to be choosing her words carefully. "Are things getting any easier, Marianne? I mean— I hope it doesn't hurt as much as it did at first."

"Well, I am getting more used to it now, I guess. There are some things that still bother me a lot. But I'm glad that Brian—and the other boys—were spared. I try to think about that whenever I get feeling low."

"That was a wonderful thing your son did. I've heard the story, but I don't think I really understand it. Marianne, how did he find his way out of that cave?"

"Jamie could always find his way home," she answered simply.

Marianne took advantage of a lull in the conversation to put the cello away. "Excuse me," she said as she lifted the big instrument off the floor and put it back in its case. "I need to put my cello away before someone steps on it. But please keep talking. This will only take a minute."

There must have been something in the way Marianne walked or the way she looked that caught Candi's attention. After Marianne had finished putting the cello away and had returned to the sofa, Candi turned to face her and looked into her eyes. "Marianne," she said boldly, "I have to confess that I've been kind of worried about you. Knowing you as well as I do, I thought you might take Jamie's death pretty hard. And now, when I see you, I'm more concerned than ever."

Marianne turned her face away from Candi's gaze and looked down at the floor. "Please don't worry about me, Candi," she pleaded. "I'm doing okay. Really." Even as she said it, Marianne knew it wasn't true. A week had passed since Jamie's death, and she was still hurting inside. Hurting badly. She corrected her earlier statement. "What I mean is that I'm doing about as well as can be expected under the circumstances."

Candi nodded but didn't speak. There was an awkward silence, but only for a moment. Marianne looked up at her friend, and, talking more slowly and deliberately, interjected a little more of her heart and feelings into the conversation.

"Well, Candi, I guess the truth is I'm not handling this very well at all. And neither is my husband. Of course it's hard to have Jamie gone. I really miss him. That's just natural, I suppose. As if that weren't enough, Brian was in an accident a few days ago. He's okay — wasn't injured or anything like that — but the car was totaled. Then, yesterday, I hurt my back. Pulled a muscle or something. I don't think it's serious, but it's sure been hurting today. Every time I move I get this sharp pain in my back — right here." Marianne put her hand on her lower back, just above the hip on the left side. "There are so many challenges right now. It's just kind of overwhelming, I guess." Marianne leaned back in the cushions of the sofa and tried to brace her back.

Candi nodded sympathetically. "I feel for you, Marianne," she said kindly. "Life has a way of ganging up on people, doesn't it? Problems are like grapes — they come in clusters."

Marianne tried to smile, but there were tears in her eyes. "I'm trying to deal with Jamie's death," she said. "But it's so hard. Maybe if he had died from a disease it would have been easier. But the way it happened was such a shock. I've tried and tried to accept what's happened. I've tried to think it through. I've cried until I honestly don't know how there can be any tears left. I've prayed and prayed. But I just feel so empty inside."

"You know," she continued sadly, "when Jamie was alive I used to worry about him a lot — what he was eating; if he was sleeping okay; how he was feeling; whether he was learning anything. There was always something to worry about because he had so many problems. Now that he's gone, all I can think about is how unfair this whole thing is for him. Compared to the rest of us, he had so little in this life. He demanded so little. But at least, when he was alive, he had something. He had *us*. Now . . ." Marianne lowered her head. She was crying softly.

Candi was watching out of the corner of her eye. "You know, Marianne," she said, choosing her words carefully, "maybe it's better this way. After all, Jamie had a lot of challenges. Not much hope for the future. This is a pretty tough world for people who can't . . ."

Instantly, blood rushing to her head, Marianne turned on the other woman in fury. "Don't you dare say that! He had as much right as anyone to live. Maybe more. Unlike you and me, he never did anything he knew was wrong." She turned away and buried her face in her hands, sobbing audibly.

Candi drew back sharply. For several seconds Marianne could hear nothing but her own anguished sobbing. It sounded deafening, but she was powerless to stop it. All at once she felt terribly weak and vulnerable. Then she felt a hand on her shoulder. "I'm sorry, Marianne," Candi whispered in her ear. "You're right. I had no right to say what I did. Jamie did deserve to live. I'm so sorry he's gone, and I'm so sorry for you."

"I'm sorry, too." Marianne put her hand on top of Candi's and pressed it tight against her shoulder as her sobs gradually subsided. Wiping the tears away from her cheeks, she looked up into Candi's face. "I didn't mean to fly off the handle like that," she apologized. "I'm just too sensitive, I guess."

"I understand. Don't worry about it. I just hope I haven't made you feel worse by coming today." Candi stood up and began moving slowly toward the door.

Marianne got to her feet and followed Candi to the door. "No," she said, shaking her head emphatically. "I'm glad you came. I do feel better after talking to you. I really need to thank you for taking the time to come today."

"You're welcome. You're my friend, Marianne. If I can help in any way, please call me. And I really do think you'll get feeling better. These things just take time. "

Marianne took Candi's hand and squeezed it gently. Then Candi was gone. Marianne lingered at the door. Then she turned, walked slowly back to the sofa, and sat down. She made herself as comfortable as possible and tried once more to ease the pain in her back and in her heart.

◆◆◆

Brian put his book down on the end table. He took off his reading glasses, folded them carefully and placed them on top of the book. Somehow he just didn't feel like reading, so he stood up and walked across the family room. Slowly he climbed the stairs, one step at a time. When he reached the main floor he peeked into the living room. Marianne was on the sofa. Earlier she had been playing her cello, and after that he had heard voices upstairs, so she must have been talking to someone. But now she was alone, resting quietly with her eyes closed. For the moment, she looked relatively comfortable and peaceful. He decided not to disturb her.

He wandered into the kitchen and made his way to the refrigerator. Absently he opened the door and started poking inside for something to eat. He passed over the cheese and yogurt. He thought briefly of the ice cream in the freezer, but reached instead for an apple. He held the apple up to look at it, then wiped it off and took a bite. After he swallowed it he looked again at the apple. He didn't feel like eating. So he went over to the trash container and dropped the remainder of the apple in it. Then he walked out of the kitchen and down the hallway to the bedrooms.

When he passed Jamie's bedroom, Brian paused and looked inside. Everything was in place — toys on the bookshelf, clothes in the closet — and the bed neatly made with Jamie's pillow resting lightly on top.

The one thing missing was the only thing that mattered. Brian thought about the boy who for fourteen years had known no other home but that room—the boy who sat on the bed or played by himself with his toys on the floor. For a moment, Brian imagined he could see a shadowy figure standing in the corner. But he knew no one was there. Not any more. So he turned away and moved on down the hallway.

He went into the master bedroom and stretched out on the bed. He lay on his back for a few minutes, then turned over on his side, trying to get comfortable, trying to let go of the thoughts and feelings that pressed upon him. Instead, he found himself thinking again about what had happened. In his mind he relived the series of events that had culminated in Jamie's death: the camping trip; the visit to the cave; the dark hours in the bowels of the mountain; Jamie's departure from his side and from his life. He remembered his feelings when he had reached out and found Jamie gone, the panic of the ensuing search in the dark, the despair that followed. And he remembered how he had broken down and cried when Terry Dickson told him that Jamie was dead. Other than that episode in the cave and the day of the funeral, he'd managed to hold back the tears. He had stayed in control. But now he felt himself choking up.

If only he had gone straight home from scout camp. If only he had insisted that the boys not enter the cave.

But thinking about the *ifs* didn't do any good. He *had* permitted the hike to Crystal Lake and the exploration of Knobby Cave. And he had done it in good faith. He had done the best he could. There was no point in beating himself up about it. What was done was done.

Still, a price had been paid. He thought of the one who had paid the price—the boy whose life was only half a life. It didn't seem fair that one who had so little should be required to give so much.

He let himself cry. Big, tough linebackers shouldn't cry. Sensible English teachers shouldn't cry. But Brian Spencer cried. He cried for a long time. He cried for himself. He cried for Marianne. And, most of all, he cried for Jamie.

When his heart and his head were drained, he got up from the bed. He didn't feel like resting, so he paced the room for awhile. Then he went over to the desk and sat down. Idly he looked around the room. Marianne's wedding portrait was on the opposite wall, the center piece of an arrangement that also featured their marriage certificate and a recent family picture. He paused for a moment to examine the picture, lingering on the image of the boy in the middle. With some effort, he shifted his attention to the inanimate objects in the room: the dark mahogany head board, dresser, and night stand; Marianne's cedar chest, filled now with extra quilts, pillow cases, and baby clothes that had outgrown their natural function but had been retained for their sentimental value.

Leaning back in his chair, Brian turned his attention to the desk top, scanning in turn the objects that were neatly lined up along the back edge of the desk. He studied the lamp, the alarm clock, the pencil holder disguised as a German drinking mug. His eyes found the gold pocket watch. Absently, he picked it up and stared at the ancient face as he rubbed the gold case with his finger.

Something about the watch was different. At first he couldn't figure out what it was. Then he saw.

The hands were moving.

He sat up at once. Holding the watch to his ear, he marveled at the regular, consistent ticking sound. Once more he turned the face toward him and watched the tiny second hand click through a complete arc in its tiny inner circle.

The watch had his full attention now. As he looked and listened, a word came into his mind — a single word. For a moment he let it float through his consciousness. Then he spoke the word — softly, reverently, almost like a prayer.

"Jamie."

And then he understood. He knew the meaning of the watch. He knew that it was revealing more than time.

Slowly he got up from the chair. "Marianne!" he exclaimed, momentarily forgetting that she was out in the living room and might not hear him. "Look at this! The watch is running again. Jamie's watch is working perfectly now."

Cradling the gold watch gently in the palm of his hand, he hurried out of the room to find his wife.